# Seasonings

# SEASONINGS

## VANCE HAVNER

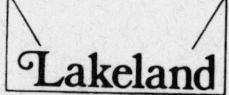

**LAKELAND**

BLUNDELL HOUSE
GOODWOOD ROAD
LONDON S.E.14

© Fleming H. Revell Company 1970

All rights reserved. No part of this publication may be reproduced, stored in a retrieval system, or transmitted, in any form or by any means, electronic, mechanical, photocopying, recording or otherwise, without the prior permission of the Copyright owner.

*First British Edition 1971*

The Scripture quotations in this publication are taken from the *King James Version of the Bible*, unless otherwise indentified.

Scripture quotations identified RSV are from the *Revised Standard Version of the Bible*, Copyrighted 1946 and 1952.

ISBN 0 551 00119 4

Reproduced photo-litho in Great Britain by
J. W. Arrowsmith Ltd., Bristol 3.

# PREFACE

I am not a maestro of the kitchen but I do know that seasoning has much to do with success in the culinary art. As a traveling preacher, I have eaten in restaurants all over America for thirty years and one need not be a gourmet or an epicure to be sensitive to too much or too little good taste in food. This goes beyond what we eat. The Scriptures would have our speech seasoned with salt. There ought to be a relish about Christianity both by lip and by life. Of course the opposite of not enough seasoning is too much and we cannot live on spice.

The tidbits recorded in this book are not meant to supplant but to supplement more solid food. They are meant to garnish the meat and potatoes. It is hoped that their purpose will be understood and accepted accordingly. There is a notion in some quarters that religious writing should be drab and that colorful language is to be avoided like a plague. The Bible is no authority for this idea for it abounds in picturesque speech. The victuals are well seasoned and appetizing. May what is written herein quicken our appetite for the Living Bread!

VANCE HAVNER

# Seasonings

# 1

Years ago in the days of the old camp meetings a preacher set out after the evening service to find his way along the edge of a dangerous cliff to the cottage where he was to spend the night. He had no lantern and flashlights were then unknown. An old farmer, sensing the preacher's predicament, lighted a bundle of pine fagots and handed them to the minister saying, "Take this, it will light your way home."

"But what if the wind blows it out?"

"It will see you home."

"But if the rain extinguishes it?"

"It will see you home."

"But what if it burns out before I get there?"

"It will see you home."

And see him home it did.

Long ago my parents put into my hands the Word of God. They told me that it would be a lamp unto my feet and a light unto my path. There have been times when the winds threatened to put out its glow and the storms seemed almost to overcome it. There were times when I was tempted to lay it down and make my way unaided. But I am almost home—and I have never been more sure of my torch. I pass it on to you. It may look old-fashioned in this nuclear age but man's little flashlights are failing fast and more poor souls are groping in the darkness than ever before. Let the critics scorn and the cynics laugh—this kindly light will lead you on "o'er moor and fen, o'er crag and torrent, till the night is gone."

It will lead you home.

Recently on a bus trip through the mountains we had a breakdown and were detained for two hours 'way back in the hills at a little grocery store. There was a woman there who was a typical mountaineer. My wife said, "She doesn't know what's going on in the world outside." I replied, "Well, *don't tell her!*"

Sometimes we drive the automobile into the repair shop and say, "Check the motor." It is time we church workers drove into God's repair shop and asked Him to "check the motive." Why do you do what you do in church?

An American teen-age tourist in Vienna went to see Beethoven's piano. She had the nerve to sit down and play some rock 'n' roll. The caretaker presently informed her that Paderewski had also visited that spot to look at the piano. "Did he play it?" she asked. "No," replied the caretaker, "He said that he did not feel worthy."

I listened to a hillbilly preacher holding forth on the radio. His text was, "And He went a little farther." Every few minutes he fairly shouted, "How fur have you went?" I was sitting there all alone but finally I blurted out, "Brother, you done went too fur now!"

"For *now* we see through a glass darkly; but *then* face to face: now I know in part; but then shall I know even as also I am known" (I Corinthians 13:12). I call that my *now* and *then* verse!

We must deal with the seeds of sin in our hearts. If neglected the seeds soon become weeds. Let us deal with the seeds and we shall have no trouble with the weeds.

Something used to happen to people from the outside when they became Christians. They were invaded from above. Now we try to work up something from the inside with a do-it-yourself religion.

# 2

John McNeill, the Scottish preacher, had some church difficulties on one occasion. Next Sunday he rose in his pulpit and said, "God and John McNeill have come to an understanding. Keep your hands off John McNeill!" The man who has settled things with God and is on good terms with the Almighty can face any situation unafraid.

Sacrilegious sinners may be more violent and vulgar but our greatest problem is religious sinners.

When I was a boy my father used to take me to an old-fashioned mill by a stream whose waters flowed onto the big waterwheel that turned all the other wheels in the mill. If the miller should discover some morning that the creek had become clogged or diverted so that there was not enough water to operate the mill, how foolish he would be to try to make the wheel go around by striving and straining to turn it in his own strength! But he could go up the creek and clear the channel, remove whatever blocked the water's flow, and then he would be in business again.

All over the land I find church workers striving to make the wheels go around. We need to go up the creek, get sin out of our lives, and remove the hindrances and debris. Then the Spirit would flow, the wheels would turn and we would have something to show for our grinding. The secret of the Acts of the Apostles was simply the inflow, the outflow, and the overflow of the Holy Spirit. Are we ready to go up the creek to make way for that inflow in our hearts and homes and churches?

You can run *from* God but you cannot run *away* from God for God is everywhere. Jonah made that discovery!

Sin has gotten man into more trouble than science can get him out of.

If Jesus came to Bethany today Mary and Martha would probably be out, and if He caught them at home they wouldn't turn the TV down low enough to hear what he had to say. At least that is the experience of visiting pastors these days!

The Scriptures speak of those who will bear on their foreheads God's name (Revelation 22:4) and also those who will bear the number of Antichrist (Revelation 13:16-18). We shall all end up among either the Named or the Numbered.

I read of a spider that tried to weave its web on the moving hands of a town clock. I do not think spiders are that stupid, but we are when we try to build our lives against the will of God, and when nations work against the moving purpose of God in history.

Two Indians watched a lighthouse under construction. On the day it opened for business a heavy fog moved in. "Ugh," said one Indian, "Light shine, bell ring, horn blow, but fog come in just the same." We have never had so many lights shining and bells ringing and horns blowing in the religious world as today and we have never had more fog!

God has done something *for* us in the gift of His Son. He wants to do something *to* us, make us new creatures in Christ Jesus. He wants to do something *in* us, working in us to will and do of His good pleasure. He wants to do something *through* us, making us His witnesses.

God had the first word with us in birth and He will have the last word in death. Both are in His hands. Blessed is the man who puts all between in His safe-keeping.

# 3

A man on trial was told by the judge: "You are entitled to have a lawyer. There is one over there at your right and another at your left and there is another out in the hall." The accused looked to the right and then to the left and said, "Your Honor, I think I'll try the one out in the hall!"

Men are looking today to the right and the left for

saviours but some of us are waiting for the Lord Himself who is out in the wings soon to return. But there is another in the hall. The grim figure of Antichrist waits there. When he appears he will not seem grim but gracious. His advance stooges are with us now, so pleasant as to make it appear evil not to endorse them. ". . . false Christs and false prophets shall rise, and shall shew signs and wonders, to seduce, if it were possible, even the elect. But take ye heed: behold I have foretold you all things" (Mark 13:22,23).

When a group of small boys, out to play ball, arrived at the playground, they discovered that no one had brought a ball. "Forget the ball," said one impatiently, "Let's go on with the game." We are trying to play without the ball when the church tries to evangelize before she has repented. The church can do many things after she has repented but nothing until first she repents.

Rudolph Serkin said of the pianist Rubinstein, now in his eighties that his music was becoming younger—almost as if he were playing everything for the first time. There ought to be such a freshness about Christians in their old age. I have heard of one who wished he had never read the Gospel of John so that he could read it for the first time! Like the saints of Ephesus we leave our first love. It need not be so with a Christian any more than with a musician.

Elijah in the cave at Horeb learned a lesson about *self-pity*. He was not the surviving saint. He learned a lesson in *statistics*. Seven thousand others had not bowed to Baal. It has been said that there are three kinds of lies: white lies, black lies and statistics. He learned a lesson in *stillness*. Man of earthquake, wind and fire that he was, he needed to hear the still small voice.

A farmer in Pennsylvania read the newspaper sermons of Billy Sunday during his great campaign there. He became convicted about his sins, packed a box of food, and took off for Pittsburgh to find out how to get saved. He missed the afternoon service on the day he arrived but met a preacher who explained the way of salvation and led him to Christ. When they rose from their knees beside the box of food the farmer had brought, he said, "Well, if I had known it was that simple, I wouldn't have brought all this week's rations along!"

After one of his great battles, Napoleon Bonaparte had coins minted bearing the words, "I Was There," which he distributed to every soldier who took part in the engagement. Could the Lord give you such a token as a good soldier of Jesus Christ? Will you be able to say when veterans tell of the great warfare, "I was there"?

". . . The stone which the builders rejected, the same is become the head of the corner" (Luke 20:17). From this text Joseph Parker preached on the stupidity of the specialists.

Sometimes on medicine bottles we read, SHAKE WELL BEFORE USING. That is what the Lord has to do with some of His saints! As the old Bible figure puts it, we are settled on our lees and need to be emptied from vessel to vessel.

# 4

Here are some trellises from my sermon garden. Some other preacher may be able to cover them with better homiletic vines than I have done. To change the figure, here are some sermon skeletons. Skeletons are important. Without them the body has no shape and cannot stand up. But there should be plenty of meat on the skeleton lest the bones be too conspicuous. Reading through a book of sermon outlines is like walking through Ezekiel's Valley of Dry Bones. They are "very dry" and one can only pray for the Spirit to blow upon them that they may live.

# "ACCORDING TO YOUR FAITH"

## "Because of Unbelief"

1. Israel was set aside nationally (Romans 11:20).
2. The generation that came out of Egypt failed to reach the Promised Land (Hebrews 3:19).
3. Christ could do no mighty works in Nazareth (Matthew 13:58).
4. Christians and churches are powerless before a demonized world (17:20).

## "O Ye of Little Faith"

1. Faith and Care (Matthew 6:30)
2. Faith and Fear (Matthew 8:26)
3. Faith and Doubt (Matthew 14:31)
4. Faith and Spiritual Stupidity (Matthew 16:8)

". . . Lord, I believe; help Thou mine unbelief" (Mark 9:24).

## "BUT AS FOR YOU. . . ."

*Perils Concerning Things* (I Timothy 6:10,11 RSV).

"But as for you . . ." (v. 11).

*Perils Concerning the Times* (2 Timothy 3 RSV).

"But as for you . . ." (v. 14).

*Perils Concerning the Truth* (2 Timothy 4:1-5 RSV).

## A TROUBLING REMEMBRANCE

"But as for you . . ." (v. 5).

"I remembered God, and was troubled . . ." (Psalm 77:3).
When I remember how holy God is and how sinful I am, I am troubled.
When I remember how good God is and how unthankful I am, I am troubled.
When I remember how busy God is and how unfaithful I am, I am troubled.

## PATTERN FOR PERILOUS TIMES

*There Is a Price to Pay* (2 Timothy 4:9-22).
*There Is a Promise to Plead* (2 Timothy 4:17; Hebrew 13:5,6).
*There Is a Prize To Possess* (2 Timothy 4:8).

## "HE HATH SAID"

*The Authority of the Promiser:* "HE hath said. . . ."
*The Authority of the Promise:* "He hath said. . . ."
*The Authority of the Promisee:* "So that we may boldly say. . . ."

## PAUL'S EXPERIENCE

*A Contact With Christ* (Acts 9:1-8).
*A Crisis With the Spirit* (Roman 7,8).

*A Contention In the Church* (Acts 15:1-30).
*A Clash With Personalities* (Acts 15:36-41).
*A Conflict in the Flesh* (2 Corinthians 12:7-10).
*A Climax In Old Age* (2 Timothy 4:6-18).

## THE LOST VOICE

"... I cannot speak ..." (Jeremiah 1:6).
"... I will not ... speak ..." (Jeremiah 20:9).
"... We cannot but speak ..." (Acts 4:20).

*Repentance is articulate* (Hosea 14:2).
*Faith is vocal* (Romans 10:9,10).
*Praise is the fruit of our lips* (Hebrews 13:15).
*Testimony is with words* (Psalm 107:2).
WE HAVE LOST OUR VOICE. WE NEED VOICE LESSONS IN REPENTANCE, FAITH, PRAISE AND TESTIMONY.

## AWAY FROM JESUS

Three men went away from Jesus
*The Great Refusal* (Matthew 19:22).
*The Great Betrayal* (John 13:30).
*The Great Denial* (Luke 22:61).

# 5

If America is not buried by Red Russia from without, we may be smothered by Red Tape from within.

I am convinced that many who attend opera and visit art galleries neither understand nor enjoy what they hear and see. They know they are supposed to and they do not want anybody to think that they do not understand or enjoy them. Likewise many churchgoers neither understand nor enjoy what they hear at church, but they want everybody to think they do. It is a matter of status and they must live up to expectations! How few worship in spirit and in truth!

Paul wrote about those who were "somewhat" up at Jerusalem (Galatians 2:6). It is easy to be awed by the "somewhats" at Headquarters.

I heard recently of an apathy protest that was called off for lack of interest!

Prophets are almost extinct in the religious world

today. The modern church is a "non-prophet" organization.

It has been said that a mark of deep spiritual maturity is to be able to enjoy the journey when God puts you on a detour.

We are hearing today about those who like Christ but do not like the church. But Christ loved the church and gave Himself for it. How can we like the Head, but not the Body, the Groom, but not the Bride?

It is time to sweep some of our pet alibis into the trash heap. For instance, "It always has been that way." (That doesn't mean it must always be that way.) "It's here to stay." (Maybe the devil and liquor and other evils are here until the end of the age, but we need not accept them, and live at peaceful coexistence with them.) "Other things are just as bad." (But that doesn't make the issue in question any better.) "It could be worse." (But it could be better.) "There's nothing you can do about it" (By that logic, nobody would ever do anything about anything!)

There is too much jumping from one spiritual experience to another, instead of abiding in Christ and abounding unto every good work.

Stardust must be mixed with sawdust—the dream

with the drudgery—if we are to translate vision into venture and live on the cobblestones what we felt among the clouds.

Some say, "If only I could have lived in Jesus' time." But plenty of people did live then and they crucified Him. Physical proximity and visibility did not help.

It used to be the Lord's Day, now it is the weekend and if we group all holidays on weekends the devil will have scored another move against Sunday worship.

We are afflicted with those dear souls who always overdo things, embracing causes so fervently that they strangle them, and driving thumbtacks with a sledgehammer.

I heard of a bishop who couldn't sleep. As the night wore on he remembered the verse, ". . . he that keepeth Israel shall neither slumber nor sleep" (Psalm 121 v. 4). He said, "Lord, if you are sitting up I don't need to, so I'm going to sleep." There is no need for insomnia if we are trusting the Night Watchman of the Universe!

A girl, critically injured in an automobile accident, said to her mother, "You taught me how to smoke a cigarette and handle a cocktail glass. What I need now is to know how to die, but you never told me that."

There is nothing morbid about getting ready to die. For a Christian, it is preparation for life's greatest adventure.

## 6

With all our time-saving devices we have less time than ever. A friend of mine visiting a nearby town was told by one of the older residents, "I used to visit your town in the horse-and-buggy days. It took me all day to do it then. Now I can come over in thirty minutes—*but I don't have time!*"

We live closer together these days—and further apart. When I was growing up in the country we knew all the neighbors for miles around. Now I don't know who lives down my street or even in my apartment house.

When we moved from the country to the city, and from the farm to the factory, we lost something we have never regained. Something happened when we began to be awakened each morning by a whistle instead of by a rooster.

Along with the air and water pollution that "progress" has created, we have the plague of noise. Man's constitution is not able to stand the racket his ingenuity has produced. He flees from the tumult to the tranquilizer.

The early church grew by *addition* (Acts 2:41,47; 5:14; 11:21,24); by *subtraction,* as in the death of Ananias and Sapphira; by *multiplication* (Acts 6:7; 9:31) and even by *division* for people had to take sides for or against as our Lord had declared (Luke 12:49-53) and the result in the long run was gain, not loss.

One serious malady of the church is infantile paralysis —too many babes who never grow.

During a Los Angeles smog one expert wrote, "Only a wind from elsewhere can dispel this condition." The world is smog-bound today and only the breath of the Spirit can relieve this fog. The church lives in a haze and only the winds of God can clear the mist. It is significant that the word for "wind" and "spirit" is the same both in the Old and New Testaments.

Our Lord practically began His ministry by cleansing the temple (John 2:12-17) and His last word to the churches was, "Repent." Spiritual awakening, like judgment, begins at the house of God.

In this day of communication and dialogue Martin Luther would be expected to work things out with

Rome. The great reformer would be reduced to a diplomat.

We hear much these days about loving our fellow men but we forget that the First Commandment is, "Thou shalt love the Lord thy God. . . ." We cannot properly love our neighbor until we love God, and we cannot love God aright until we are born again and become His children, sharing His nature. Trying to get a pagan generation to obey the Golden Rule, and an unregenerate society to abide by the Sermon on the Mount is a waste of time.

Great emphasis is being given to the pastor as the "equipper" of the laymen for their ministry (Ephesians 4:11,12). This is part of his work, but he also has a prophetic ministry which is fast disappearing as prophets become priests.

America is fractured and fragmented into hundreds of little groups wanting their own rights while nobody seems to care what happens to the country. A house divided against itself cannot stand.

# 7

When General MacArthur was driven out of the Phillippines by the Japanese invasion, he said, "I shall return," and return he did. Before our Lord left this earth He said, "I will return . . ." (Acts 15:16), and return He will. I expect to return and reign with Him on a redeemed earth. The Bible pictures of a new heaven and earth are not mere poetic imagery. In Romans (8: 18-23) Paul gives us the Christian doctrine of the place of nature in God's redemptive program. Creation groans, we groan, and the Spirit groans as He prays for us—but groans will one day give way to glory. We shall return to earth when Christ rules it for a thousand years, and then to a new earth which, along with the new heaven, will be our abode forever.

If experts could do it we would have had a revival long before now. We have had conventions, conferences, symposiums, panel discussions, books, magazine articles, sermons galore on the subject—but no revival. One of these days God will step in and say, "You fellows have tried long enough . . . I'll take over." He may begin in a way that will upset all our nice calculations, embarrass the avant-garde boys, and turn the faces of the specialists a bright red. He may start in some little country church out at Frogpond, or across the sea or with some other race or denomination than yours. May we be Christian enough to welcome the breath of the Spirit, no matter from which direction the breeze may blow!

I read a fable about a nightingale that offered a fisherman a feather each day in return for a worm. As time went on the nightingale, bereft of feathers, could not fly. He asked the fisherman to reverse the arrangement and trade back feathers for worms. "No," was the reply, "I only trade worms for feathers." The man who gambles with the devil will find that it is a one-way deal.

There is not much connection between what most of us do at church on Sunday, and the way we live the rest of the week.

One might change the old poem a bit and say that the Christian's main business is to be occupied with *the wrong that needs resistance, the cause that lacks assistance, the future in the distance, and the good that we can do.*

One frequently meets passersby with music emanating from transistor radios on their persons. Lacking music in our hearts, we carry it in our pockets!

The trend today is away from God. The Christian must beware of endorsing anything which, though there may be reasonable argument for it, actually contributes to the trend, the drift, the movement of the age, or which at least gives that impression.

Somebody asked Grandfather, "Do you sleep with your long beard under the covers or outside?" He hadn't really given it any thought. That night he tried sleeping with his beard under the covers and couldn't sleep. Then he tried it outside the covers and fared no better. He lost a whole night's sleep over a foolish question that didn't matter. Hours have been wasted over other issues just as unimportant.

Old Samuel Shepherd said, "The truly godly are not sad because they are too godly but because they are not more godly. They have grace enough to bring them off carnal and worldly delights, but not enough to enable them to live upon the spiritual and eternal world, and to fetch all their comfort from there." This accounts for the serious demeanor of great souls in contrast to the tra-la-la spirit of the happiness boys.

# 8

In the days of Constantine, the church controlled the culture of that day. Today the culture of this age is in the hands of the world. We are in the grip of worldwide paganism, and the true church is an alien minority. The professing church has been so assimilated by the age that it has little influence in this day and generation. Some churchmen would have the church try through education, reformation, and legislation to control the present order. But God never meant for the church to overcome the world that way. Constantine did not Christianize his day, he merely "Constantinized" it. Trying to Christianize paganism he paganized Christianity. Christians are the salt of the earth, and we are to permeate and infiltrate it, but the world will never be converted. It ought to be evangelized, but its set-up will not be Christianized. God never started out to do that to begin with—He is taking out a people for His Name. The sooner we find that out, and get busy with God's program instead of human projects under religious auspices, the better it will be for all of us.

A well-known football team was criticized for running out the clock in the last minutes of the game. The score was tied, and they played safe, taking no chances with the ball lest the opposing team grab it and score in the very finish of the battle. We are not in life's game to lose or to tie, but to win. The tendency today in Christian warfare is to play safe, and take no chances rather than risk everything in an all-out fight for victory. We do not confront the forces of evil in a head-on collision. We settle for a draw. We hold summit conferences with the world, the flesh, and the devil. It is the new age of peaceful coexistence. The Word of God knows nothing of such third dimensions where we neither win nor lose. There is no substitute for victory. There is only the alternative, defeat.

On that great day of Peter's confession in Caesarea Philippi, four mighty issues were set forth (Matthew 16:13-28). First, *The Christ* of Peter's confession (v. 16). Then our Lord spoke of His *church* (v. 18). Next, He spoke of His approaching death and discipleship, the *cross* in its double aspect, our Lord's cross and ours (vs. 21-26). Finally, His *coming*, His return (v. 27). Was more ever crowded into a few verses?

The Bible records one long continued clash between institutionalized religion and the prophet. Whether it be Elijah and the false prophets, Micaiah and "the Four Hundred," Amos and Amaziah, or Lord and the Pharisees, the story is the same. That conflict has raged through the centuries since. Today religion was never more organized, but prophets are scarce. The voice of dissent is pitifully weak as the age of regimentation homogenizes the race for the mark of the Beast and Antichrist. Amos is ordered out of Bethel by Amaziah and his little religious empire. John the Baptist is still no favorite in the courts of Herod. And the path of the greatest Prophet of all leads to a cross.

It is a day of fading declarations. The old Declaration of Independence lies faded in Washington. America has become a disaster area in its family life because too many marriage certificates are fading in their significance. Church covenants are found in the backs of hymn books, but they have faded in the lives of most of our members—if they ever meant anything. The Bible itself is a faded document as it lies dust-covered in many a home. Preachers' ordination certificates have faded in their meaning along with the experience that gave them birth. Declarations of personal dedication grow dim, and need to be renewed. It is a day of faded declarations!

# 9

It is said that during a coin shortage, Oliver Cromwell sent some of his men to one of the cathedrals to look for metal to be made into money. One of them returned and reported, "The only silver we could find is in the statues of the saints." "Good," replied Cromwell, "We'll melt down the saints and put them into circulation!" How the saints need to be melted today into God's spending money!

". . . This is the victory that overcometh the world, even our faith" (I John 5:4). We do not think in terms of victory nowadays. Wars are fought to a draw, a stalemate—we neither win nor lose. We are afraid to win, and ashamed to lose. We follow the same policy in spiritual warfare. We play for a tie, and we fight to a draw. It is about time we went in to win.

"And in the morning, rising up a great while before day, he went out, and departed into a solitary place, and there prayed" (Mark 1:35). Our Lord found both time ("a great while before day") and place ("a solitary place") for prayer. We are hard put to it these days to find either, but find them we must for what we are at prayer is what we are and nothing more.

Mary was supposed to be doing her music lesson. Everything seemed unusually quiet. Mother asked what was going on, and Mary replied, "I'm practicing the rests!" Christians need to practice the rests which may be as important as our work.

When Abraham's servant was ready to start for home with Isaac's bride-to-be, her brother and mother said, "Let the damsel abide with us a few days, at the least ten; after that she shall go." Realizing the danger of delay the faithful servant gave an answer that should be on the lips of every Christian when threatened by the clever delaying tactics of the devil, ". . . Hinder me not, seeing the Lord hath prospered my way" (Genesis 25: 56).

Repentance is not a mere change of opinion. It is a complete change of inner attitude toward sin and self, and God. It amounts to nothing if it does not produce fruits meet for repentance. The step must be followed by the walk. The Prodigal Son did not merely come to himself and say, "I will arise and go to my father"—he went! There is nothing meritorious in faith or prayer or repentance save as they connect us with God. They are but means to an end, and have no value in themselves.

I remember seeing a picture of the Roman Colosseum with this beneath, "This is the Roman Colosseum where the early Christians died for the faith *which we now take for granted.*" We take for granted the beauty of creation, the common pleasures of life and our ability to enjoy them, and health and friends and family; we take America for granted, and the church as a matter of course. Few of us would want to live where there are no churches, but most of us live *as though* there were no churches. We take our faith for granted, and what we take for granted we never take seriously.

Some say we should not dwell on the soiled garments of the church, but rather magnify the dazzling robe of our Christ. But we are not only to put on the Lord Jesus Christ, we are told, ". . . make not provision for the flesh . . ." (Roman 13:14). Indeed, we should preach grace, but remember that grace teaches us to deny ungodliness and worldly lusts. True, we should preach the promises as well as the commandments of God, but remember that having these promises, we should cleanse ourselves from all filthiness of the flesh and spirit. ". . . The Lord knoweth them that are his" (2 Timothy 2:19), but they are exhorted to depart from iniquity.

We work hard and get little done in church today because we are chopping with a dull axe. Yet we refuse to take time out to sharpen the axe. No time is lost when we are sharpening the instrument.

# 10

The vision must be followed by the venture. It is not enough to stare up the steps—we must step up the stairs.

Our heads are traveling by fast express these days, and our hearts follow by slow freight.

It is debatable which is causing us more harm—hot-headed ignorance or cold-hearted intellectualism.

Paul advised Timothy: "Let no man despise thy youth" (1 Timothy 4:12). It is possible to despise one's own youth. We can reach that sad day when we look down with scorn on earlier years when we started out all aglow with first love before grim reality smothered our zeal. Once lost, that exuberance is rarely regained.

Maturity can mean several things. Physically, beyond maturity we reach old age and die. Unless we live again in our children the race is soon extinct. Maturity can lead only to the mortician and the mortuary and the mausoleum! Unless the church is renewed, her boasted maturity leads only to Laodiceanism.

Men do not feel their need of God nowadays because they look to the labor union for retirement benefits, to the government for hospital care, to wonder drugs for their ailments, and to tranquilizers for comfort. A pill averts consequences of immortality. Man is now his own judge of what is right and wrong. He has just about given God His walking papers.

Our Lord made it clear that many would appear at the last day who had prophesied, cast out demons and done many wonderful works, only to be told, "Depart from me, ye that work iniquity [lawlessness]" (Matthew 7:21-23). Mind you, there will be *many*—not just some—such preachers and they are called workers of lawlessness. Here is a frightening possibility that deserves more serious attention than it has ever received.

My father lived in a day when an honest man's word was his bond. Dad never made much money, and was no haberdasher's model, but his word was respected over at the little county-seat town twelve miles away. If he said he would be somewhere on Monday morning at ten he didn't mean eleven-thirty, and if he promised to pay a debt this week he didn't mean the middle of next week. Of course he would be a square today when there are more clever ways of getting on in the world. Dad did not know the tricks of the go-getters, and would be smiled upon with condescending tolerance as an outmoded specimen. He was just plain honest, and honesty is a rare commodity today. He knew nothing of the art of double-talk from both sides of his mouth. He never left you guessing as to what he meant, and he did not have two lines of comment, one to your face and another to your back. It is appalling how dissimulation flourishes in Christian work nowadays. We need not gaze afar with a telescope trying to locate causes for the churches' lack of power. Part of it can be found close at hand in men—sometimes prominent—who do not keep their word and whose sincerity is dubious. We could stand plenty of old-fashioned dependability, rugged integrity, and unpretentious honesty in the church today.

It would be foolish for a man too sick to do his normal work to argue, "But at least I'm getting a few things done and I don't have time for a check-up and maybe surgery." It is just as foolish for sick churches to avoid self-examination and spiritual surgery by arguing that at least some souls are being won, and that they are still in motion. It is not good to carry on trying to act well when we should admit we are sick—and do something about it.

# 11

The first business of the church is not to evangelize, but to be ready to evangelize. We are trying to excite an unprepared, undedicated mob of church members to rush out into a business for which they are not ready in mind or heart—a Gideon's thirty-two thousand utterly without training, for the most part of a carnal mixed multitude marching out to spiritual warfare of which they know nothing, and for which they could not care less. The first item on our agenda is to produce a better grade of Christians before we go out to add more names to our church rolls when we already have too many of the kind we have. We need seriously to ponder our Lord's words to the Pharisees: ". . . ye compass sea and land to make one proselyte and when he is made, ye make him twofold more the child of hell than yourselves" (Matthew 23:15).

It is seriously to be questioned whether we can have deep conviction, conversion or consecration in a generation as shallow as this. Long ago our Lord told us of the shallow soil, of those who receive the Word with joy, but have no root or depth, and are easily offended by trouble or persecution. A generation that lives on the surface as we do today provides no fertile soil for a deep work of grace, and will produce a poor harvest.

Years ago during a war two ships glimpsed each other in a fog and fired at each other for an hour. When the fog lifted they discovered that both flew the same flag! Many a battle in the history of the church has resulted from mistaken identity in a theological fog.

The best way to detect counterfeit money is not by studying all varieties of bogus currency, but by becoming so well acquainted with the genuine that we can instantly spot the false. One could spend a lifetime in the study of false cults and isms and never come to the end of it. Rather let him come to know his Bible and his Lord so well, that no false Christ can lead him astray. Knowing the Shepherd's voice, he will not heed the voice of strangers.

A woman in a white dress was denied entrance to a coal mine she wanted to explore. "Why can't I wear a white dress into the mine?" she asked. "Lady," replied the gate man, "There's nothing to hinder you from wearing a white dress *into* the mine but plenty to keep you from wearing a white dress *out* of the mine." ... "All things are lawful," (1 Corinthians 6:12) but many things are not expedient; they do not edify and they may enslave us. We do not come out as we went in, and our garments are spotted.

Some are looking *for* Jesus—questing for the historic Christ. Some are merely looking *at* Him as a model, an example. The Christian looks *unto* Jesus for salvation and everything else.

We can go to the mission field in *person*, by *prayer*, by *provision*, or by *proxy* as we help send someone else. But there is a mission field across the street as well as across the sea. And perhaps the most urgent mission field right now is the membership of the average church.

Our greatest failure is in the follow-up. We take a step of consecration, but do not follow it with a day-by-day walk. Churches have revivals, but lapse back into the same old rut as before. We reason that one cannot live in such rarefied spiritual air the year round. Our problem today is what the Scriptures call "patient continuance" (Romans 2:7). ". . . if ye continue in my word, then are ye my disciples indeed" (John 8:31). The truth sets us free, but only as we continue in the word. It is freedom through faith that follows! Our failure as Christians and churches is in the follow-up. There are not many advanced students in the school of Christ because there are too many dropouts.

## 12

The Pharisees had many good points. Our Lord said, in effect, "Do as they say." They read the Scriptures, prayed, went to God's house, tithed, and lived separated lives. They were anxious to preserve religion in Israel. Winning converts to the religion of Moses had been a good and right thing to do. But their religion had become institutionalized, and now they were propagating a dead faith and every new convert was a twofold child of hell, a lost heathen and a lost proselyte. Generally, we are propagating today a degenerate brand of Christianity. Unless the church repents, and has a complete overhauling instead of a tune-up job, our evangelistic and missionary drives may add for the most part only a multitude of proselytes who are both unsaved pagans and regenerated church members. Like produces like. Worldly churches produce more worldly members. Churches weak or unsound in doctrine produce more of the same variety. Churches that operate in the energy of the flesh instead of by the Holy Spirit produce more of the same kind. We must improve the present quality of our churches, for converts tend to take on the qualities of the people who convert them.

Some preachers ought to put more fire into their sermons or more sermons into the fire.

If I stood on a street corner selling fine watches for a dollar apiece, I could work up a crowd and have a following, but I would still have to settle with the watch company. If I preach a cheap Gospel I may build up a crowd, but I must give account to God for my message.

Some people do not have much trouble with the devil. They are so worthless he doesn't waste time on them.

We have too few Calebs and Joshuas and too many scared spies with a grasshopper complex. The ten cowards said, ". . . we were in our own sight as grasshoppers, and so were we in their [the Canaanites] sight" (Numbers 13:33). That figures. If we think we are grasshoppers, others will make it unanimous.

We commemorate great spiritual events of the past, but we do not duplicate them. It is one thing to celebrate Aldersgate; it is another thing to feel our own hearts strangely warmed.

What is sometimes thought to be firm conviction may be just simple obstinacy.

We have enough chain logic in our preaching; what we need is chain lightning!

We are in a day of nice preaching. Sam Jones and Billy Sunday would horrify our delicate tastes nowadays, which is rather strange considering that our tastes for books, music and television programs are not exactly refined. Apparently we want elegance in the pulpit, but elegance has not always been the pulpit tradition. Amos at Bethel and John the Baptist in the wilderness would hardly qualify. The New Testament is not a textbook for the dainty elegance school. Its language is not classical Greek but the speech of the marketplace: "... generations of vipers" (Matthew 12:30), "... dead men's bones ..." (23:27), "... go tell that fox ..." (Luke 13:32), "the sow ... [has returned] to her wallowing in the mire" (2 Peter 2:22) and "I will spue thee out of my mouth" (Revelation 3:16). They don't add up to sermonic lullabies! It's about time for some robust colorful preacher to recover the lost weapons of sarcasm and satire, and deal with the devil's imps as demons, not as daffodils.

It may take all kinds of people to make a world, but it would be a better world if we had fewer of some kinds of people.

## 13

When our Lord walked on the storm-tossed waters He did not say, "It is morning, it is fair weather, there is no storm." He said, ". . . it is I" Mark 6:50).

The cause of broken marriages is selfishness in one form or another. Change one letter in the word "united," and it reads "untied." And that letter is "I"!

An optimist is a man who thinks the preacher is nearly through when he says, "Finally. . . ."

When the spiritual temperature of a church is high enough it will kill all the germs.

God preserves the saints, but He does not pickle them.

There is not necessarily more strength in numbers. A hundred blind men can't see any better than one blind man. Uniting two or three sects that have lost their faith does not help. Two or three times nothing is still nothing.

Some missionaries bound for Africa were laughed at by the boat captain. "You'll only die over there," he said. But a missionary replied, "Captain, *we died before we started*."

Some of our brethren believe that it is possible for a Christian to lose his salvation. It has been said, "A Methodist knows he has religion but is afraid he may lose it; a Baptist does not believe he can lose it but is afraid sometimes that he doesn't have it." Sam Jones, the great Methodist evangelist, was talking with a friend when a small dog rushed by, chased by a larger dog. The second dog was being chased in turn by a still larger dog. Sam Jones pointed to the middle sized dog and said, "He's just like a Methodist. A Methodist has to run like everything because he's got heaven before him and hell behind him!"

Some churchgoers are human wet blankets, and would chill whatever warmth might be in a meeting. They are like the brother who mixed his figures of speech in his prayer and said, "Lord, if there should be a spark of fire in this service, please water that spark!"

If a school required no study of its pupils and passed the students regardless of performance, it would soon be held in contempt. A church that holds no standards of doctrine and exercises no discipline soon loses the respect of even the ungodly.

I read of an old mountaineer who had spent almost all his life before a great mountain he had never climbed. One day a friend took him in his automobile up a new road to the lofty summit. As the old man surveyed the glorious view in all directions, the tears coursed down his weatherbeaten face and he managed to say, "Just think, I lived in sight of this peak nearly all my days, and almost missed it!" It is possible to live all of one's days close to great truth and never see it.

The devil's strategy today reminds us of the Viet Nam war. There is no front line now. The world has infiltrated the church until it is honeycombed with unbelief and worldliness. The enemy is all around us, behind us, and beside us. All this talk about joining hands, closing ranks and marching ahead overlooks the nature of our conflict. Christians, the salt of the earth, should permeate society, but the professing church instead is being permeated by the world and molded by the age. Issues are no longer clearly defined, and we are in guerilla warfare. The traitor in our ranks is more dangerous than the enemy ahead. These are extremely weird and strange times, and the rules of ordinary procedure do not cover the situation.

## 14

If all things work together for good to God's people, then a Christian cannot take a turn for the worse. It can be said of every child of God who dies, that he took a turn for the better. ". . . to depart and to be with Christ . . . is far better" (Philippians 1:23).

Sam Jones said that when asked about finances in his earlier ministry, he always replied, "I leave that with the bretheren." Sam added, "And I really did, for when I left the brethren still had it."

I'm awfully tired of hearing temperance in liquor drinking preached instead of abstinence—as a concession to the cocktail crowd in the congregation.

We are being told today that men do not go to hell because of their sins, but because they did not believe in Christ. Rightly understood, this is true, but if a man dies with pneumonia refusing to have a doctor, it may be true that he died for lack of treatment, but he still died of pneumonia.

"Join the church of your choice," is standard advice for young converts today. But that is good only if their choice is God's choice. Many young converts do not know how to choose the right church. They need guidance and instruction in choosing a church where the Word of God is preached and taught, where there is warm Christian atmosphere for spiritual growth, and opportunities for definite service. Some churches do not qualify on these points.

"A man is not a sinner because he is a drunkard; he is a drunkard because he is a sinner." This is true but such statements sometimes indicate a leniency toward liquor and the liquor business. It can be expanded to cover all forms of evil and can be misconstrued to encourage a light regard for all forms of iniquity. Such pronouncements are often part of the stock in trade of modern tolerationists who make sin appear less sinful. It is about time we brushed up on the First Book of Corinthians chapter six, verses nine and ten.

Cancer can often be cured in its early stages, but the chances are slim when the case is advanced. Many evils could be handled if detected and dealt with in their incipiency, but the man who cries out at sin in its beginnings is called a witch-hunter, a viewer-with-alarm. There is hope when we put the finger on sin at its start, but when it becomes malignant in the individual, in the church, and in society, it is often too late to do much about it. There is always hope, but the victims are usually hardened and next to impossible to treat. Small sins in personal living, worldliness in the church, and false doctrine in theological schools—all these yield to early treatment better than later radical surgery, but woe to the troubleshooter who spots them early and points them out!

## 15

"You are playing the notes, but not the music," said Pablo Casals to his cello class. One thinks of the Psalmist, "Thy statutes have been my songs in the house of my pilgrimage" (Psalm 119:54). It is possible to have the mandates without the melody, the lawbook without the songbook. The Pharisees were experts in the letter of the law, but they had not the spirit of it. The letter kills, but the spirit gives life. The church at Ephesus was still playing the notes, but not the music—the first love was gone. Many a sermon is correct in its facts, but utterly without fire. The notes but not the music! It is the sad state of a Christian when the joy of salvation is lost. It is the plight of a church where there is plenty of theology but no doxology. The score may be correct, but the performance is cold. It is important that we play the right notes, but God save us from the tragedy of notes without music!

We need a Fellowship of First-handers who have had an original personal experience of Jesus Christ. Like the Samaritans who believed in Him, not because of the testimony of another, but for themselves—like the poor sick woman who pressed through the crowd to touch the Master for herself. Too much Christian experience today is second-hand. Blessed is the man who gets tired of books and sermons and explanations and interpretations, and simply trusts Jesus for everything. He thus cuts a knot which he might be all his life unraveling.

I am disturbed by some winds that blow across evangelical Christianity today. I listen and watch and read and hear great argument about relevance and dialogue and involvement. I wade through seminars and panel discussions and symposiums where intellectuals high in the theological stratosphere hold forth in terms unintelligible to men of low estate who are without benefit of encyclopedias, lexicons and German dictionaries. My soul hungers like the old Dutchman who sighed, "I sure vould like to get into a good old Jesus meeting." I am not longing for the good old days because some of the good old days weren't so good. It is not old age for younger preachers confide to me the same yearning. Some of them came along in the last years of the earlier period and are painfully aware that something has departed. Some dear bretheren who once were warm and who could stir up the gift within us have grown so polished that they sparkle, but while our eyes blink in their brilliance—they do not fill with tears. We have looked into our own hearts to make sure that the trouble was not with the receiver instead of the transmitter, but we notice that (to change the figure) the coals in our hearts still glow when the Spirit breathes upon them. There is a sizable number of us who think we would enjoy attending an old-fashioned brush-arbor camp meeting long enough to get the taste out of our mouth which the new school has created. It is hard to find the precise words to describe our nostalgia. It is better "felt than telt." Some readers will understand. There are some who still preach to that need and bless our souls, and not all of them are in *Who's Who*. It is that indefinable something that does not always accompany pulpit fame or great learning, although it may sometimes. Not much of it is being generated in the schools of the prophets these days. A Ph.D. does not guarantee it. While evangelicals are blowing out fuses trying to be intellectual and discussing "trends" and "thrusts" and "approaches," there are some country preachers at whose feet we could sit with profit.

## 16

One of my boyhood memories is that of my father sitting up late on Saturday before the fourth Sunday of the month talking with the minister who always spent that night at our house. They did not gossip—they talked about the things of God. I remember my farmer friend, John Brown, in my first pastorate. He came to my room about once a week to talk long and late. I remember our family physician who was never in a hurry. The night my father died the old doctor sat with us for hours. People had time in those days. Now we have time-saving gadgets galore—and we have less time than ever. What doctor has time to sit a spell? How many ministers can stop their breathless dashing from Dan to Beersheba to be still and talk awhile? We have never been busier and with less to show for our busy-ness. Television is lord of our evenings and when have you seen anybody strolling along in meditation? The Frankenstein we have created with our technology has devoured us. The very devices that were intended to give us leisure have destroyed the capacity to enjoy that leisure. And what holds more terror for us moderns than solitude, since we cannot endure our own company!

The law is fulfilled in loving God and one's neighbor as one's self. To love one's self aright is to seek the highest good, and that highest good is the will of God. We seek the most money, pleasure, and fame for ourselves but not the highest good. To love one's neighbor as one's self, it follows, is to seek his highest good as well as ours. But so to love God, self and others is not possible to the natural man. Only the twice-born new man can do it, and that love is shed abroad in our hearts by the Holy Spirit. Our part is to consent and cooperate.

A little boy at church had no money to put into the offering. He wrote, "I Give Myself," on a piece of paper and put it in the collection plate. That is the gift God wants first and most. The Macedonians first gave themselves, then service and substance. Have you ever put yourself on God's collection plate?

Those who compromise with the world in order to get along say sometimes, "But I must live with my contemporaries." Yes, but a man must also live with his conscience, and when a man lets the vices of his contemporaries dull the voice of his conscience, he has struck a poor bargain in the popularity he may gain.

Dr. Torrey used to say that the chief purpose of

prayer is that God may be glorified in the answer. "Father, glorify Thy name . . ." was the prayer of our Lord when His soul was troubled (John 12:28). It ought to be our prayer when we are troubled and know not what to say.

A picture of Christ was hung in the back of a pulpit. When the minister rose to speak one Sunday morning, a little boy asked his mother, "Mother, who is that man who stands so we can't see Jesus?"

"He that saith"—PROFESSION
"He abideth in Him"—POSITION
"Ought . . . so to walk"—PRACTICE
"As He walked"—PERFECTION

Zacchaeus was "up a tree." God knows when you are "up a tree." Zacchaeus was an onlooker and a spectator, but Jesus made him a participant. There are too many spectators up a tree these days where Jesus is passing by, and not enough who will sell out and join His party.

# 17

Of all the illusions, phantasms and farces of human history the biggest is the mirage we call progress. Just because we have split the atom and have reached the moon, we have given God His walking papers, have decided that we can work out our own salvation and that science can answer the problem of sin. The Scriptures tell us that history will end in catastrophe, abounding lawlessness and abating love—perilous times in a world that has lost its way. There is not one area today —government, law observance, common safety, morality, the national debt, world peace, air pollution, water pollution, the traffic problem, art and literature, family life, theology, you-name-it—there is not one area that is not one hopeless mess. "Even so, come, Lord Jesus" (Revelation 22:20).

I read of a doctor who took a stand on a certain medical issue that was laughed at by his contemporaries in the profession. But ultimately it turned out that he was correct. Someone, said, "He was wrong so long that he turned out to be right." Some of us have become accustomed to the ridicule of swivel-chair experts in eschatology. One of these days when God splits the skies, when the stars fall and the moon turns to blood and men cry for rocks and mountains to fall on them, some of us will have a hard time to keep from saying, "I told you so!"

One of the passengers in a terrible train wreck was a physician. As he moved among the injured and dying, he kept moaning, "If only I had my instruments!" He was a physician by profession, but for want of equipment he could do little practicing. We are living in a wrecked world. We who are Christians by profession are often limited in practice by lack of tools. Our chief instrument is the Word of God and woe unto the Christian who is not well enough acquainted with it to know how to use it!

Said Timorous to Christian," The farther I go, the more I meet with." Do not think for a moment that the Christian way grows easier as we go along. God may test experienced saints with trials He would never send on beginners. It is the battle-scarred veteran who is given the toughest assignment. Consider it a promotion if you are laid aside or not allowed to do the big thing you had hoped to do. He may have for you a greater thing in teaching you patience and endurance. There is no comfortable retirement in this conflict. Do not count on a pleasant repose to cushion your last years. Sometimes it is so, but God does not guarantee it. There will be plenty of time for that hereafter. Paul's last letter to Timothy was not written from a cottage in a balmy clime—it was penned from a Roman jail.

Chrisitianity is not being *applied* to this age but *adapted* by compromise with the world, the flesh and the devil.

Our newer hymnbooks leave out the fifth verse of Charles Wesley's immortal "O For A thousand Tongues." For some reason they stop short with the fourth verse and one looks in vain for those lines that burst with old-fashioned camp-meeting exuberance:

> Hear Him, ye deaf; His praise, ye dumb,
> Your loosened tongues employ;
> Ye blind, behold your Saviour come;
> And leap, ye lame, for joy.

Could it be that we have grown so stiff and starched in spiritual experience that we frown upon the idea of leaping for joy? The lame man in the temple gate gave Peter and John a *look*; he received a *lift*; with the lift came *life* in his ankle bones and he *leaped* for joy. Early Methodism shook England with common people fairly dancing for delight in heartfelt religion. The staid Dr. R. W. Dale, dignified Congregationalist that he was, told a congregation of Methodists in 1891 in City Road Chapel in London that their *Amens* and glad outcries of

*Glory to God* and *Praise the Lord* carried home the Gospel to the hearts of multitudes. He said further, "It was largely in the strength of your testimony to the witness of the Spirit that you won your early triumphs. If your faith in this doctrine ever declines you will lose your preachers." Think it over. Other people besides Methodists need not only to put the leap back into Wesley's hymn but into their hearts.

# 18

Some can relate clear-cut definite personal experiences, pinpointing the exact time of conversion or a later filling of the Spirit, dramatic instances of healing, guidance, striking cases of answered prayer and Divine intervention. Others are not so favored, but spend all their lives simply "looking unto Jesus" for everything. They have no spectacular episodes to tell. Sometimes they hear others recount amazing encounters with God, and are beset with doubts about their own condition. They may seek earnestly for similar experiences without success. He is a wise man who simply trusts and leaves the manifestations with God. The soul that simply looks away from all else, even its own tears and prayers and efforts and feelings and trusts Christ for everything, resting on the Word of God as the ground of assurance, *that* soul knows what our Lord meant when He said, ". . . Blessed are they that have not seen and yet have believed" (John 20:29), and what Peter meant when he wrote, ". . . in Whom, though now ye see him not, yet believing, ye rejoice with joy unspeakable and full of glory" (1 Peter 1:8).

The experts tell us that in a few more years we shall have to wear gas masks on account of the polluted air, and hearing aids on account of the noise. Add to that all the other gear we shall have to carry on account of "progress" and a Martian would be a tame sight compared to your ordinary citizen of the "Golden Age" supposed to be just ahead of us.

There is much confusion about the difference between deciding and doing. The prodigal son decided to arise and go to his father, but we read next that he arose and came to his father. These are not the same thing. Plenty of decisions are made that never amount to anything. One of the sons in our Lord's parable, told by his father to go work in the vineyeard, said, ". . . I go, Sir," (Matthew 21:30), but he went not. Through the years I have seen hundreds of people come down church aisles making "decisions" who never do anything. If all the young people who have decided to be missionaries had become missionaries, the world would have been evangelized long ago. Crisis is not followed by continuance. The step does not begin a walk. There is a sort of satisfaction in having done what the minister asked by "coming forward" but it is not followed by going onward.

My father used to say that Dirt, Debt and the Devil were related. I have always felt that they belonged in the same family. The Bible takes a dim view of debt. I realize, of course, that it is now part of the American way of life. The government is the chief of sinners leading the way with staggering obligations that will never be paid. Any man who tries to pay cash for a house or an automobile is viewed these days as a curiosity—a throwback to some prehistoric era. I know the experts and loan companies look with condescending pity on any poor square with ideas as out of step with progress as mine. I never owed but three hundred dollars in my life. I borrowed it as a boy in order to go to school, and was nervous until I paid it back. I still believe that any man who manages to get through this benighted age of progress owing "no man anything but to love one another . . ." (Romans 13:8), is on the best side of the argument.

# 19

It is true that what shuts a man out of heaven is unbelief. That, however, should not shut our mouths from preaching, at the proper time and place, about other sins. After all, Paul did not write, "Unbelievers shall not inherit the kingdom of God . . ." Indeed they shall not, but Paul specified a formidable list, ". . . Be not deceived: neither fornicators, nor idolators, nor adulterers, nor effeminate, nor abusers of themselves with mankind, Nor thieves, nor covetous, nor drunkards, nor revilers, nor extortioners, shall inherit the kingdom of God" (I Corinthians 6:9,10). Instead of generalizing on sin we need to particularize, and do some plain and powerful preaching on all the evils Paul enumerated. The devil has cleverly silenced the pulpit my misusing the proposition that unbelief is the sin that damns the soul. We have never had such a superabundance of fornicators, idolators, adulterers, homosexuals, perverts, drunkards, thieves, swindlers, foul-mouthed and robbers as now, and the increase is due in no small part to the fact that all these have been accepted into society (yes, church society) and given status by a degenerate Christianity that is long on tolerance and short on truth.

Many God-fearing people, distressed by the times, are keeping silent because they do not wish to be identified with extremist groups that happen to hold some of the same beliefs. They are embarrassed by some outfits they wouldn't be caught dead with who agree with them on some points. The devil believes there is a God. So do I and I am not going to keep quiet about my belief in God because the devil happens to be of the same mind on the matter. It is a shrewd device of Satan to shut us up on vital issues by parading disreputable radicals who loudly proclaim some of our beliefs in order to further their cause.

The prophet is a troubleshooter, not a troublemaker. Ahab asked Elijah: ". . . Art thou he that troubleth Israel?" (I King 18:17). But Ahab was the real troublemaker as Elijah promptly informed him. Elijah was the troubleshooter. When evil conditions arise in the nation or in the church, God raises up a prophet. He is not a pastor, teacher or evangelist. These function when the machinery is running smoothly but when evil days come, we need prophets. The supply is low today. Prophets are very disturbing to smug church members who like to sit half-asleep in church on Sunday morning while the minister drones platitudes that offend nobody. Industrial organizations call in troubleshooters to find bugs in the set-up, locate the trouble and prescribe the remedy. Why shouldn't the church welcome prophets? The prophet has a genius for locating trouble and a gift for exposing it. That makes him unpopular with resters-at-ease in Zion who think he ought to act like the non-irritating, inoffensive brand of clergymen. They are utterly mistaken. A prophet is not a priest.

We face three tests in our journey here below. There is the test of the miraculous, the *marvelous*, the great days when we are on the mountaintop of great success. It takes special grace for that because we tend to grow proud and drunken with the wine of victory. There is the test of the *monotonous*, the daily grind, and it takes great grace for the weeks and months when nothing much happens and life sinks into routine. But the greatest test is the *mysterious* chapter, when things happen that don't make sense, when God seems to have forgotten us, when nothing works out according to all our little plans—and when instead of a storybook ending, all crashes in unexplainable confusion. Paul knew all three chapters—the third-heaven exaltation, the daily care of the churches, the thorn in the flesh. Blessed is the man who is fortified by a double dose of Divine grace for the *marvelous*, the *monotonous*, the *mysterious*.

# 20

Some years ago I visited a Northern city in early spring. I knew where I was going so I wore my winter overcoat. When I arrived at my hotel the sun was shining and the weather was pleasant. I looked decidedly out of place in the lobby dressed for winter in the throng of convention delegates. But next day it turned cold. I sauntered into that shivering crowd envied by everybody who had left his overcoat at home. This was my day!

The Christian who prepares for the coming of the Lord may be scorned by all who say, "Peace and safety!" He will be eyed as a curiosity by those who, like people of Noah's day, know not until the flood comes. But when God splits the skies and the stars fall and men cry for the rocks and mountains that will be his day!

Jonathan said to David, "I will be next to thee" (I Samuel 23:17). The rarest man in the orchestra of God is the saint who knows how to play second fiddle.

If things are quiet and undisturbed in your church, that is not necessarily a good sign. Things are usually pretty quiet around the sick and the dead and especially in graveyards.

I am not *dead* sure about the doctrines of our faith, I'm *alive* sure! There is too much dead orthodoxy already; we need living convictions.

The new pitch some experts in Christian witnessing use is to say; "I want to tell you what a wonderful life you can live as a Christian." But the Book of Romans begins with a fearful chapter on the depravity of the human heart. John Bunyan said that when God tunes an instrument He begins with the base.

They tell us that we must not begin by quoting Scripture, but by telling our own experience. I seem to remember something about faith coming by hearing and hearing by the Word of God.

It is next to impossible to find a quiet place for meditation these days. If you do not carry a calm spot in your soul, it will not help much to find one on the outside.

It has been said that Patrick Henry asked, "Give me liberty or give me death," but modern Americans simply say, "Gimme." Certainly in this day of the welfare state Uncle Sam has become our Santa Claus. Christians make a Santa Claus of God and praying is usually a long list of "gimmes" longer than a small boy draws up before Christmas. How few can say:

> Once earthly joy I craved,
> Sought peace and rest;
> Now Thee alone I seek,
> Give what is best.

In a Roman jail an old preacher wrote to his son in the Gospel to bring ". . . [my] cloke and . . . parchments" (2 Timothy 4:13). He had no stocks except those around his feet and no bonds except those he wore on his wrists. All he wanted in life was to know Jesus Christ, the power of His resurrection and the fellowship of His sufferings. God was not merely his Rewarder, God was his Reward.

Paul had gotten over the gimmes!

Using Christian terminology means nothing if one is not a Christian. Having a case of athlete's foot doesn't make you an athlete!

# 21

It might be a shocking discovery that going to church can be a sin, but it is a frightening possibility. In Isaiah God declares that incense is an abomination to Him, and that His soul hates new moons and appointed feasts when men do not worship Him in Spirit and in truth. Since God hates only evil, we may well ponder whether much of our Sunday morning Christianity may be sinful if it is not spiritual. It might stun some churches that pride themselves on their beautiful music, orderly services, clever sermons and attendance records to hear that all this can be disgusting to God, even as Laodicean lukewarmness nauseated our Lord. Ritual without reality, performance without experience, a form of godliness denying the power thereof,—all this not merely vain, it is downright evil and instead of being gloried in, it should be repented of. Amos blasted it in Bethel, and the Saviour Himself denounced the religious institutionalism of His day. If a prophet stood in some sanctuaries on Sunday morning and called our so-called worship what some of it really is, the congregation might feel insulted and the prophet might be escorted from the pulpit, but he would be walking in good Scriptural succession. We had better wake up to the fact that we are deceiving nobody but ourselves. Even the world knows the difference between force and farce, and certainly God is not mocked.

A ship is safe in a harbor but ships are made for the seas. Harbors are not only destinations for incoming ships, they are ports from which ships go out. The church is indeed a haven where weary souls may come for strength and comfort, but churches are also starting points from which we go out to serve. It has been said that the Gospel is not merely something to come to church to hear; it is something to go from church to tell. Too many smug Sunday morning churchgoers never dream that they were meant to go out of church to practice what was preached inside.

One writer tells of an old lady who always began her testimony at prayer meeting by saying, "Forty years ago . . . ." The writer says, "I felt like asking her, 'Lady, hasn't anything happened since?'" We thank God for the happy day that fixed our choice on Him our Saviour and our God, but there should be more happy days all along. Christian lives sometimes become like some married lives that get to where there is nothing left but anniversaries.

Recently a visitor was being shown around in a new church building. "This church is so well insulated," he was told, "that no sound can be heard from outside!" Too many churches are so insulated that they never hear the call of a dying world.

It has been pointed out that the human race has not increased merely because God said, "Be fruitful, and multiply and replenish the earth . . ." (Genesis 1:29). God planted a biological urge within man and the population increase came naturally. Our Lord told us to go make disciples, but Christianity's gains have not been merely a compliance with that command. The fruit of a Christian is another Christian and there should be within us a burning desire to win others to our Lord. The growth of the church should be not only obedience to a command, but the outworking of a compulsion.

Judas bought a field with the reward of iniquity (Acts 1:18). Barnabas sold a field and laid the money at the apostles feet (Acts 4:36, 37). Annanias and Sapphira sold land and kept back part of the price (Acts 5:1-11). What a man does about his real estate is a pretty good index to his real state.

## 22

Revivals should not be necessary. God never meant that His people should live by fits and starts in alternate periods of backsliding and reprenting. But since we have such "malarial" Christianity (a fever and a chill, a fever and a chill) we shall have need of revivals. If we walked with God and kept ourselves prayed up, it would not be necessary to call in preachers every six months to stir up the church. If we had more "vival" we would not need re-vival. We would live in normal spiritual health all the time without shots in the arm twice a year.

My father was faithful the year round. It did not require a talking horse or religious movies to attract him to the house of the Lord. He did not have to rededicate every few months like those who spend their time shuttling between Bethel and Shechem. He stayed dedicated. He had a "vival" and didn't need re-vival.

Agrippa "got the message" when Paul preached to him. "Are you trying to make a Christian of me?" Paul was not out merely to defend himself, but to win his listeners to Christ and His cause. Is that the objective of your testimony? Does your message end with one point like a sword or does it end like a broom with a thousand straws?

Most of our evangelism today is not reviving the church. Converts are won and members are added, but the churches go on pretty much the same. Nor does our evangelism make much impact on entrenched wickedness in the city. There was a time when revivals closed saloons, shook up the dens of evil and made the devil mad. Nowadays we do little more than provoke a yawn. Our cautious approach with preaching guaranteed to offend nobody, generalizing on sin but never daring to particularize, and aiming at peaceful coexistence with the devil's crowd instead of a head-on collision—this strategy is not disturbing the strongholds of organized iniquity. We capture a convert here and there, but there is no frontal assault and pitched battle on the main line.

One of Satan's most effective weapons is "Trendism." (There is no such word but when I cannot find a word I need I make one.) Trendism is this business of studying and following the trends of the times, carried away with every wind of doctrine, "getting with it," drifting with the drift, following the crowd, and swept along by the current. Trendism is the order of the day, and we are a generation of Trendists. The man of God was never meant to catch the spirit of the times, but to condemn and correct it. He is not to be a chip carried by the current, but a rock jutting out into the stream around which the waters boil because it cannot be moved.

Many things may not be evil in themselves when taken out of their context. Meat offered to idols was not inherently evil, but Paul saw it in its context and would not touch it. The real test of any issue is, *what is it a part of? whither does it tend? what wave is it riding?*

The time to cry out against evil is when it begins. Churchill says Communism should have been strangled at birth. If we wait until false doctrine or worldliness are entrenched, it is too late. We must nip them in the bud—kill the little snake before it becomes a boa constrictor. Nobody dares warn against the early symptoms of moral malignancy. Such a prophet is called a calamity howler, a witch hunter. But the true shepherd sees the wolf *coming* and does not wait to act until the wolf is in the midst of the flock.

## 23

Strange notes are being sounded these days in the world of Gospel music. We are hearing that if an African convert wants to express his religion in jazz, let him bring his drums to church. Maybe rock 'n' roll can be used to praise the Lord! Jazz bands now perform in staid old churches. Once we took the church to the jungle; now we take the jungle to the church. All of this is but a symptom of the degeneracy of these days—the moral malignancy that approaches its terminal stage in a nation not yet two hundred years old. When the night club invades the sanctuary it ought not be difficult for any Bible Christian to discern the time of day.

Church discipline is being revised to omit all reference to such matters as drinking and dancing. It may be best to deal in principles rather than particulars but the worldly majority in our churches uses that argument to erase all lines of demarkation between the church and the world. The trend is toward lawlessness—the breaking down of discipline in the home, government and church—and anything that relaxes our standards is part of that trend. It is true that Christians should be guided by general New Testament principles, but the average church member is so ignorant of the New Testament that we have to spell things out. Parents should be guided by certain general principles, but they often have to be very explicit. ("No, you cannot do that!") The breakdown of our homes today is due to the surrender of discipline in order to go along with the trend. Most church members are babes in kindergarten, and must be dealt with as such. Generalizing must be implemented by particularizing.

Almost everybody these days is discussing what's wrong with almost everything. There is plenty to talk about for there is plenty wrong, but for a change somebody ought to talk awhile about what's right with something. There is much that is wrong in America but there is much that is right. We have our glorious heritage, and there are many, both in Washington and outside, who love this land and are good Americans. There are boys who will die for their country, and a grass-roots multitude of plain folks who have not bowed to Baal. There is much wrong with our homes and too many weddings that are not marriages, but there are still dads and mothers who are true to each other, who have family prayers and are trying to bring up decent children. There is plenty wrong with teen-agers, but I have met a host of red-blooded, good-looking youngsters who have high ideals, work hard and really want to be good

Christians. There is much wrong in the church, but there are plenty of churches where the Gospel is preached and souls are saved and where faithful preachers who never get any publicity are shepherding their flocks seeking only the Chief Shepherd's, "Well done." It's about time we asked ourselves: "Am I contributing to what's wrong or what's right? Which side has my vote?" Any morning-after quarterback can sit around and gripe about how the game ought to have been played, but we are short on volunteers who show up for practice.

Above all, there is One about whom there is nothing wrong. He asked, "Which of you convinceth me of sin?" (John 8:46). What are we doing about Jesus Christ? Let a man get rightly related to Him and he will be a good American, a good husband, a good teen-ager, a good church member. The man who never definitely lines up with what's right, is definitely lined up with what's wrong. He is a part of the problem when he ought to be part of the answer. There are no innocent bystanders these days, for if a man is a bystander he's not innocent. Our Lord said, "He that is not with me is against me; and he that gathereth not with me scattereth abroad" (Matthew 12:30).

## 24

Some things can be explained today by the fact that this generation is growing up before a TV screen instead of an open fire.

It is not always a sign of church progress when financial receipts go up. Giving a little more money may be a neat way of salving our consciences. The Macedonians first gave themselves. Self, service, substance is the Divine order and nothing counts until we give ourselves.

We are challenged these days, but not changed, convicted, but not converted. We hear, but do not and thereby we deceive ourselves.

The church, instead of relaxing her standards to please worldly members, ought to set them so high that it pulls us to our full height to live up to them. When we loosen our discipline for popularity's sake—when we are more interested in the approval and support of the worldly than in their spiritual welfare—we may build a big church, but it will not be a New Testament church—only a religious club under religious auspices. We are like those misguided fathers who in trying to be pals with their children lose their authority as parents.

Someone has outlined the Twenty-Third Psalm this way:
   WITH ME—The Good Shepherd
   BENEATH ME—Green Pastures
   BESIDE ME—Still Waters
   BEFORE ME—A Table
   AROUND ME—My Enemies
   AFTER ME—Goodness and mercy
   AHEAD OF ME—The House of the Lord

There is a set up for you! What is there to fear when a man is that well situated! As an old Scotsman put it: "Whoever heard of anybody drowning with his head that high above water!" No wonder a little girl began the immortal Psalm: "The Lord's my Shepherd—that's all I want!"

Too many Christians and churches want to settle for a tune-up job when they need an overhauling.

We are easily deceived by massive church buildings, impressive statistics, and Sunday-morning church attendance. Actually much of this gigantic build-up does not mean much today. It makes little real impact on this generation. We are thankful for the blessings and by-products of Christianity, but real Christians are a minority group in a pagan land even in America. The church is not molding the community, it is being molded by the community. There is so much unbelief, worldliness, strife and confusion that, for the most part, only a diluted Christianity remains—a form of godliness without power. God is moving today in the narrow stream of the faithful remnant: the seven thousand who have not bowed the knee to Baal.

I like to stroll in cemeteries. They do not depress me. At least they are quiet and nobody talks back! This afternoon on my graveyard stroll a couple of bluebirds came along. One perched on a tombstone and favored me with his ethereal warble. The monument spoke of death and dissolution; the bluebird spoke of life and resurrection. One marked the end of life, the other a new beginning. Old winter may still bluster and blow, but the bluebird tells me that a gentler springtime is on its way. There's more to a bluebird than meets the eye!

## 25

Mrs. Woodrow Wilson tells how her mother's old cook said to her on her wedding day as she and the president came down the stairs, "Take Jesus for your doctor and your friend." Mrs. Wilson adds, "Many times since, I have thought that if I could take Him with as simple and childlike faith as this fine old black woman did, the new life with its broader opportunities could have been more enriched for myself and more useful to others."

". . . every one of us shall give account of himself to God" (Romans 14:12). The student must face examinations and give account of how well he has used his time and done his homework. We must give account to the government at income tax time. The salesman must turn in his report to the boss. Why should it be thought a strange thing that we mortals must give account to God for the deeds done in the body—the way we have spent our lives? We have a date with Diety, an appointment with the Almighty. It may not be on our little note book of engagements, but it is on *His* schedule!

Often I see the words, "Christ Is The Answer." Indeed He is the answer to everything. If we are Christians we are members of His body, and therefore part of the answer. But judging by the way some Christians live, they are part of the problem!

The simplest joys are the sweetest, and some of the memories that linger longest are of little things. To this day I remember waking up at the old home in the country on my first morning back from boarding school. It was springtime. The bees were buzzing in the blossoms of the apple trees around the house. The birds were in full song, the flowers fresh, and the air warm and clean. I couldn't wait to take off and explore my old haunts in the woods and old Shep was all set to go along. It was in the very last days before the First World War, and it was a world we lost never to regain.

The New Testament requires that those who minister in church be good men filled with the Holy Spirit. Eloquence alone does not qualify the preacher, artistry the soloist or business experience the deacons. A church greeter at the front door may grin like a Cheshire cat, but what lies back of the grin? Every activity of Christians in the church and outside the church should be the outflow and overflow of the inflow of the Holy Spirit.

A trainer of Seeing Eye dogs distingushes between mistakes and basic faults in dogs. The application extends to us humans. Everybody makes mistakes and they should be corrected, but far more serious are basic faults that require uprooting at any cost. Carelessness, dishonesty, moral laxity, intemperance in any form—any fundamental defect—must be dealt with rigidly in its early stages. And by no means is such an elemental weakness to be classed with the occasional mistakes we all make.

NOTE TO MINISTERS: There is a world of difference between a sermon on your mind and a sermon on your heart—between getting things off your chest and pouring out your heart—between carrying your church on your back and carrying it in your heart.

The Rich Farmer in our Lord's parable had the wrong clock. It said, "Many years," but God said, "This day." Be sure your timepiece is set with God's. More important than daylight saving time is soul-saving time!

## 26

When John F. Kennedy rode along the streets of Dallas on his assasination day bystanders must have felt that he "had it made." Young, educated, wealthy, and with an attractive wife and family, he was President of the United States and a world figure. But a rifle cracked and all that mattered was how things stood between John F. Kennedy and God.

> The boast of heraldry, the pomp of power,
> And all that beauty, all that wealth e'er gave,
> Await alike the inevitable hour.
> The paths of glory lead but to the grave.

But whether rich man, poor man, beggar man, thief, it always comes to how things stand between us and God. But why wait until then? That is all that matters anytime!

The weather, like everything else in creation, was wrecked by the advent of sin. How perverse and lawless it can be! One day is like Paradise and then comes murderous flood, earthquake, hurricane to slaughter the innocent and sweep away earth's most treasured possessions. Unpredictable, the despair of the forecaster, treacherous, one day lion, the next day lamb, like our own human nature, the weather is an example of the disordered by-products of the advent of Satan. He is the Prince of the Power of the Air and uses the weather often to his purposes as he did with Job long ago. But Satan can go no further than God allows him, and one day he will be cast out of his domain. Fortunately man does not yet control the weather, else it would be in a far worse state. But one day it will be part of the Peaceable Kingdom where nothing shall hurt or destroy. That ought to be a blessed day for all weather forecasters whose faces stay red so much of the time these days.

Paul had a desire to depart and be with Christ. The type of saint who is homesick for heaven is pretty scarce these days. There is nothing morbid or abnormal about such a longing. The average Christian has driven down his tent pegs in this world, and is so comfortably settled in these lowlands that heaven does not have the attraction for those pilgrims and strangers who look for a City which has foundations whose builder and maker is God. It is difficult to stir up any excitement about the world to come in a generation as earth-bound as the present crop of mortals. The emphasis today is on the church in the world, and we are not only in it but of it. It sounds almost corny to sing "In The Sweet By-and-by." We are too busy living it up in the Here and

Now. How many church members do you know who give you the impression of being travelers through this world headed for a better country? In this affluent age it is next to impossible to create any heavenly longings in Laodiceans rich and increased with goods and needing nothing. Heavenly homesickness! When have you seen any symptoms of that blessed ailment?

Christian lives do not always end in storybook fashion in happy final chapters where everything comes out just right. Some do spend sunset years in pleasant circumstances of peace and comfort, but others—just as saintly—end in suffering and grief. Indeed, veterans who have fought long against the powers of wickedness may wind up with a sort of shell-shock paying a toll in body and mind for daring to challenge the demons of darkness. Some of God's best go home in the dark, and the last round may puzzle those who worship the god of Happy Endings. Our Saviour did not spend His last days in the serene enjoyment of friends—a benign Galilean philosopher. He went out on a cross in agony beyond words with the world turned black. We had better not expect much of this age, but be prepared for anything. Paul did not come to the finish in a placid setting. We shall be in for a rude awakening if we do not understand the nature of spiritual warfare in this world.

## 27

Long ago I read a story that I have never seen since, but have never forgotten. An Indian chief called his warriors and said to them, "I want you to climb yonder mountain peaks. You may not reach the summit, but wherever you stop, pick up something to bring back that I may know how far you went. If you reach the top you will glimpse in the distance the shining sea." They went, and when they returned one by one, the first brought a sprig of pine, another a twig of fir. Late in the evening the last warrior reported. His hands were empty. "Why have you brought nothing?" demanded the chief. "Where I was, there was nothing," was the reply, "but . . . *I saw the sea!*"

Paul had little in his hands to show at the end of life's journey. The men who have climbed highest usually show fewest visible tokens. Their reward is within. *They saw the sea!*

One would think that Christmas and Easter would be the best seasons for church revivals, but nobody dreams of trying it at Christmas, and the Easter crowd is hardly in the mood. Plenty of churchgoers are ready to take part in the Palm Sunday parade and the Easter celebration, but will have nothing to do with Gethsemane and Calvary in the week between. They join the multitude in welcoming the Saviour into Jerusalem, and they observe His Resurrection on the next Sunday, but they will not go with Him through the garden to Golgotha. Now of course our Lord trod the way of the cross alone for only He could die for our sins. But all true Christians were buried and rose with Him and can say with Paul, "I am crucified with Christ . . ." (Galatians 2:20). Before we can work this out in its daily application, we must first be ready to say, ". . . not my will, but thine, be done" (Luke 22:42). Alas, how few of our church people know anything about that! Indeed, too many who join that welcoming multitude on Palm Sunday shout with that other throng a few days later, "Crucify Him!" These Palm Sunday and Easter celebrants are often enemies of the cross of Christ and put Him to an open shame.

Once in a while God creates a prophet, and He begins, as with Jeremiah, before his birth. Such men have a special and peculiar attitude toward many things. They have slight regard for forms and ceremonies, are disgusted with the age they live in, and are disturbing to all who seek only to preserve the status quo. They are misfits in the order of their times, and probably nobody misunderstands them more than the contemporary clergy. Amaziah is horrified by Amos at Bethel. They are anathematized in their day—and memorialized a generation or so later. Their motives are maligned, their messages scorned, and their manners ridiculed. They are a strange and solitary breed with few intimate friends, and are driven thereby to a close walk with God. Lean and hungry, they belong like eagles to the crags and not to cages. They are without honor in their own house, as the greatest of them said, ostracized by the religious establishment, and feared by evil men in high places. For the work of a prophet let no weaklings apply. For that sort there are comfortable posts with fringe benefits and old age security assured. For the prophet there are the ravens of Cherith, the widow of Zarephath and the hatred of Jezebel. But of all men, these successors to Elijah know how to sing at the finish, "Swing low, sweet chariot." Prophets cannot be produced in run-of-the-mill schools; they are born with a bent ordained of God—a makeup that is the despair of all preacher-makers on the conventional assembly lines. Nobody understands them but God, and often they are driven almost to despair under the juniper. Only God knows what to do with a prophet. History owes an incalculable debt to these Lone Dissenters, and it will be paid in the coin of the age to come of which they preached, and for which they lived.

# 28

Edison failed in many of his experiments. Lincoln failed to get elected to several offices before he became president. There is a difference between failing and being a failure. There is a difference between the traveler who stumbles on the journey, and the man who never starts or gives up when he falls.

I believe it was S. D. Gordon who was riding along in the cotton country back in the horse-and-buggy days, when he passed a cabin where an old black woman sat serenely on the little porch. He called across the cotton patch, "Auntie, do you live here all alone?" "No, suh," she replied, "just me and Jesus." He said, "I drove a ways down the road, took off my hat, knelt in the buggy and prayed, 'Lord, help me so to live that when people pass my house they may be able to say, S. D. Gordon lives here—and Jesus.'"

It was decided in a certain family that there should always be one chair at the head of the table, which was never to be occupied by any member of the family or a guest. It was the Lord's chair, to remind them always that He was present with them. Sometimes father would come home tired and maybe a bit irritable; maybe mother would be worn by the end of the day or the children difficult some mornings, but always the chair reminded them of Another no less real although to sight unseen. Maybe it would be a good idea for all of us to set up an extra chair!

If I've heard it once, I've heard it countless times, "It all depends on how you look at it." Nothing depends on how we look at it. That would be the last verse of the Book of Judges all over again with every man doing that which is right in his own eyes. That is anarchy, with every man his own judge, and we are in the midst of that sad state today. Everything depends on how *God* looks at it, and what He says about it in His Word.

I started out preaching as a lad, and Father used to meet me at the little railroad station of the nearest town when I returned home. I can see him now, standing beside the old Ford in his blue serge suit that had not been pressed since he bought it. Always his first word was, "How did you get along?" The years have passed, and I still recall those days when I pass the little old station still standing. One of these days I expect to make my last trip, and end up in glory, and I am quite sure that among the first to greet me will be Father. I am also quite sure that his first word may be, "How did you get along?" I think I will answer, "Quite well, and much of the credit goes to you for the life you lived, and the start you gave me."

In the spring the birds come through, but the average American cannot identify a dozen kinds of these visitors in the trees. Yet we are surrounded by them, singing for all who have ears to hear. I am not an expert bird man, but even I can identify over fifty by their song alone, and I mean the songbirds, not birds of prey, or game birds, or water birds. God speaks to us in many voices: in Scripture and prayer, and events and books, and music and friends, but too often, *hearing, we hear not*. Our Saviour knocks at the door for anyone who will hear His voice. If you practice listening for birds, you will hear them, and scores of bird songs that others never hear. If you listen for God with a heart that says with the boy Samuel, ". . . Speak, Lord, for thy servant heareth . . ." (I Samuel 3:9), you will hear Him.

# 29

Puzzled and perplexed, church leaders are asking today, "Where do we go from here?" Frankly, we are not going anywhere until and unless we do something about here. Where we are is no place to take off from. Joshua tried to go on from Jericho to Ai in the conquest of Canaan, but was defeated, and would have been defeated again if he had not dealt with sin in the camp, and evil in Israel. Until the church deals with sins in her membership, she is not ready for any forward march. We assume that everything is in good shape in our own ranks, and plan ambitious projects and programs, and set fabulous goals. But we cannot get there from here until we do something about ourselves where we now are.

Seen on a church bulletin board: "It takes no musical ability to be always harping on something!"

A grindstone will either dull or sharpen an axe. It depends on how you hold the axe. A Christian's testimony is either dulled or sharpened by contact with the age in which he lives, depending on how he meets it.

## "IFS" OF REVIVAL:

*Confession* (2 Chronicles 7:14).
*Separation* (I John 2:15).
*Submission* (Romans 10:9).
*Filling of the Spirit* (John 7:37-39).
*Continuance* (John 8:31).

Savonarola, Huss, Cranmer—these and many others took a stand for God that cost them their lives. We are heirs to their legacy. There would be no vital Christianity today if they had chosen the line of least resistance. Today some feel that the Reformers should have worked things out at a conference table. Luther should have chosen peaceful coexistence. The new pitch is to go along, and achieve our goals by being politicians instead of prophets. We are trying to untie knots we should cut. But the situation grows knottier. It is the day of Erasmus, not Luther and one thing is certain—the new angle isn't working. The new reformers are too proud to admit their failure.

France spent millions on the Maginot Line, but Hitler simply circumvented it, and it was rendered useless. The church has reared her fortifications, but the devil is giving us the runaround these days. Modern spiritual warfare is not a matter of frontal assault. The enemy sneaks in, outflanks us, infiltrates us. Right and wrong do not clash in head-on collision. Maginot Lines do no good if we are not alert to the strategy of the runaround.

We call this an age of progress, but when I was a young man I could walk in Central Park, New York, in peace and safety, and women could stroll down Washington streets at night without fear. It can't be done now. Will some of the pointers-with-pride please explain?

G. K. Chesterton pointed out the wisdom of our jury system. He said that when we want a library cataloged or a solar system checked we call in experts, but in determining the guilt or innocence of a man, we call in twelve ordinary men. He adds that the same thing was done by the Founder of Christianity. If I were on trial I wouldn't want twelve experts on the jury. They'd hang me for certain. I'm glad the Lord didn't choose twelve theologians. He picked ordinary fishermen, tax gatherers, and the like. The average man is a better risk than the expert. He often arrives by intuition and common sense at a conclusion it might take some Ph.D's months of study to reach. The common people heard Jesus gladly. Not many wise, mighty and noble are called. When Castro started his revolution in Cuba, plenty of plain people could have told you he was a Communist, but it took the experts, including some church leaders, a long time to find it out—or at least to admit it. If our only hope today lies in the intellectuals and the specialists, we are sunk.

# 30

Somebody has said, "If you must drown, don't drown in a mud puddle!" If you must fail, go down in a big cause. There are men who ought to be battling lions who spend their days swatting mosquitoes.

Too many professing Christians want sunbaths when they need surgery. When our Lord commanded that we cut off an offending hand or eye, He was using striking language to say that whatever causes us to offend others is not to be treated lightly. There are too many adhesive strips and not enough operations.

When we deplore violence, but allow television to pour it into our homes hour by hour—when we lament highway slaughter, with not a word about the liquor business that is responsible for more traffic deaths than any other single cause—when we worry about lung cancer, but tolerate tobacco—when we moan about crime, while criminals are coddled and the courts shackle the police—anybody with horse sense and a stable mind knows this is simply a matter of trying to mop the floor while we leave the faucet running.

We are trying to put a new robe on the prodigal while he is still in the pigsty—trying to give him a new ring while he still feeds hogs—trying to kill the fatted calf for him before he has ever come to himself. The orginal prodigal did not say, "I will arise and apply for government aid." He was not rehabilitated until he returned to the father.

If you try to be everything to everybody, you will end up being nothing to anybody.

If liquor is to be made, it certainly ought to be produced on a creek hidden from view. We have dignified it and given it status by putting it in fancy stores on Main Street. It belongs in the gutter and the swamp and in the dark, as part of the world of evil which is its native habitat.

Too few of the Lord's soldiers will be decorated for extreme bravery under fire. Most of them nowadays will be known only for extreme caution under cover.

Noodles have no individuality. They have to be mixed with chicken or soup—nobody eats a plain bowl of noodles. We have a lot of spineless noodle Christians these days. I'd hate to be a noodle!

We are trying to create an ideal social order than can exist only when Christ returns. The church is a soloist, not an accompanist, and was never intended to play second fiddle to political projects disguised as moral issues. Christians were never intended to become involved in trying to superimpose a counterfeit millenium upon an unregenerate world.

We have never had so many social and political and ecclesiastical surgeons working on humanity as today. The trouble is, the operations are brilliant but the patient is dying.

Too many churches are like a big electric sign with most of the letters out. We need to be plugged into the socket of Divine power. No wonder the world can't read what we are trying to say.

# 31

". . . Can God furnish a table in the wilderness" (Psalm 78:19)? ". . . From whence can a man satisfy these men with bread here in the wilderness" (Mark 8:4)? When our Lord fed the multitude there was *a bread problem*. There was *a budget proposed*—Philip "made an estimate" that two hundred pennyworth of bread would not feed such a crowd. There was *a boy presented*—Andrew, always introducing somebody to Jesus (the Greeks who came to see Him, his brother, Peter) said, "There is a lad here." There was *a bounty provided*—plenty of food with basketsfull left over. When God provides there is always a surplus, for He giveth liberally.

*What to do in Rome*: we may have to live in Rome but we don't have to do as Rome does. There is a message to proclaim in Rome (Acts 28:23). There is a life to be lived in Rome (Romans 1:7,8). There is a fellowship to be cultivated in Rome (2 Timothy 1:17).

We have a threefold *commission*—to a *bewildered*

*church,* typified by the disciples after the resurrection (Mark 16:7)—to *backsliding Christians,* like Peter after his denial (same verse)—to a *benighted world* (Matthew 28:18-20).

## DO YOU KNOW JESUS?

Are you convinced about Him? Are you committed to Him? Are you conscious of Him? (Romans 10:17; II Timothy 1:12; John 14:21).

## GOD'S CURE FOR IGNORANCE

Romans 11:25; I Corinithians 10:1; 12:1; I Thessalonians 4:13; II Peter 3:8).
*The World Does Not Know its Peril* (Matthew 24:39).
*The Church Does Not Know its Need* (Revelation 3:17).
*Christians Do Not Know Their Lord* (John 14:9).
*Sinners Do Not Know the Saviour* (John 4:10).

## FOLLOWING ON TO KNOW THE LORD
### (Hosea 6:1-3)
*A Heavenly Promise: "Then shall we know...."*
*A High Pursuit: "If we follow on...."*
*A Holy Purpose: "To know the Lord...."*

We are bought with an infinite price (I Peter 1:18,19). We are beset by invisible powers (Ephesians 6:12). We are blessed by an invincible Presence (Hebrews 13:5,6).

Paul exhorted Timothy as to *doctrine* (I Timothy 4:

13,16), dynamic (II Timothy 1:6), and discipline (II Timothy 2:3).

"I have seen servants upon horses, and princes walking as servants upon the earth" (Ecclesiastes 10:7). How often have incompetents sat in seats of power, while truly great men have held lowly stations! The ministry has often seen mediocrity elevated to top seats in the synagogue, while pulpit princes have pastored country churches. *Equestrian Servants And Pedestrian Princes!*

". . . As he is, so are we in this world" (I John 4:17). *"As He Is"*—Not as He *was;* *"So are we"*—not "so shall we be" or "So should we be"; *"in this world"*—Not just in church. His life is our life; His joys are our joys; His sorrows are our sorrows; His friends are our friends; His future is our future.

## HINDERING SPIRITS (Matthew 13:58).

The Fighting Spirit
The Frivolous Spirit
The Fed-Up Spirit

The church is not witnessing miracles today because of contention, belligerency, lack of love—by flippancy that makes light of holy things—by self-satisfaction, surfeited and gorged by too much of everything—except what we need most.

## 32

When one of the cameras on *Apollo 12* failed, it became necessary to simulate the activities of the astronauts for the television viewers. As I watched this acting out of what we could not actually see, I was reminded of how much of our religious life today is simulation—playacting—a form of godliness without the power. Our Lord called it hypocrisy. Religious drama and movies simulate spiritual experiences, and so do many churchgoers on Sunday. The Pharisees were experts at it, and our Lord spoke of preachers at the last great day who will have prophesied, done many mighty works and cast out demons, only to be declared "workers of iniquity."

True Christianity must be *vital* —it must have life. It must be *vocal*—it must be an articulate faith. It must be *visible*—showing up in daily conduct. It ought to be *vivid*—glowing, not pale and colorless. And it ought to be *victorious* for ". . . this is the victory that overcometh the world, even our faith" (I John 5:4).

Those who say that hippies with their beards and long

hair look like Jesus, make me think of one preacher's experience. After his dedication he smoked for awhile, and justified it by saying, "Spurgeon smoked." He said the Lord answered him by saying, "Yes, and that is the only way you are like Spurgeon!"

Recently I watched a concert where famous violinists, pianists and vocalists performed. Their teachers were shown in the audience. The teachers were not celebrities, but they rejoiced in the reflected light of their past students. Well may a servant of the Lord rejoice, if he can train someone who may outshine him in the public eye.

The ministry of a prophet may not seem to accomplish much. God told Isaiah to go ahead and preach, but that nobody would do what he said. He said the same thing to Ezekiel, but added, "They shall know that a prophet hath been among them" (Ezekiel 34:24). We are not responsible for what our listeners do about it. Our business is to proclaim the message faithfully, and our reward is that our listeners shall know one day that a prophet was among them.

There is one thing worse than not coming to church, and that is to come and do nothing about the message one hears. James tells us that hearing without doing means self-deception.

Some say that to believe the Bible miracles would mean intellectual suicide for them. If all who complain that way did commit such suicide, it would not be a major disaster!

Reuben was described by his father as being "Unstable as water . . ." (Genesis 49:4). Water follows the line of least resistance. It freezes over at a certain temperature, and boils over when overheated. It fits into the shape of any receptacle. It seems that Reuben transmitted his characteristics to his descendants, because in Judges we read that the Reubenites did not go to battle with Deborah and Barak—they preferred safety listening to the shepherd's flutes at home to the dangers of following the trumpets of war. We are oversupplied with Reubenites to this day.

We have gone off the deep end on education. Will Rogers said, "I don't know how we'll find jobs for all these college graduates if we eighth-grade failures don't help them out." If everybody becomes a Ph.D, who'll collect the garbage?

# 33

We hear it said, "There is nothing unusual about the revolt of modern youth. Young people have always been in revolt. We have always had crime and lawlessness." But something new has been added these days. We are not seeing ordinary meanness, but intensified evil as Satan heats the furnace seven times hotter. There is a concentrated double-distilled spirit of Antichrist in the world. This is demonism in the guise, not only of Communism, but of a dozen other evils in one final big drive before the V-Day of our Lord.

If God ever visits us again in real revival, there will be many red faces as churchmen and religious leaders blush and hang their heads in shame for the silly and stupid ways in which we have tried to promote the work of God in the energy of the flesh by the help of the world. Drama will be unnecessary. We may not even need great preachers! Gospel jazz will slink away, and we shall be chagrined that we ever sank so low as to tolerate it. All this will vanish in the blinding light of the holiness of God, and no flesh will glory in His presence.

At a much-publicized trial recently there was so much testimony by experts in unintelligible terms, that the judge dismissed it all and told the jury to use their own intelligence! This procedure ought to be duplicated in more places than courts nowadays.

Amos did not get a return invitation to Bethel. He wasn't even invited the first time! If he preached in some of our convocations nowadays, he would be escorted from the platform.

The ball player who fails to touch first base is "out," even though he circles all the bases. If you are not born again, the Great Umpire will rule you out even though you made a home run as a church member.

Daniel Webster attended a church outside the capitol because, as he put it, "In the city they preach to Daniel Webster the statesman, but this man preaches to Daniel Webster the sinner." Christ died for sinners, not for lawyers and doctors and engineers and financiers—just sinners. And we come to Him on the same ground, just as we are without one plea, just as sinners. He devoted that sacred head for *sinners* such as we. He came into the world to save *sinners*. He was called Jesus, because

He came to save us, not from poverty or from ignorance or from the ghetto, but from our sins. Sin must be dealt with first.

Too many church members wear fancy uniforms, but don't know how to play the game. They look good in a dress parade at Easter, but they smell the battle afar off.

I heard a preacher brother tell about a little girl who climbed a tree, but couldn't get down. She called on her smaller brother to pray. He prayed the only prayer he knew, the one he had been taught to use at meals, "Lord, we thank Thee for our food. . . ." When he finished, the little girl lost her grip and hit the ground. She jumped up and yelled, "Stupid! You prayed the wrong prayer!"

An angel opened the doors of the prison, but Peter was on his own when they got out. An angel directed Peter to the house of Cornelius, but Peter had to tell the Roman how to be saved. We need to learn the lesson of the Departing Angel.

# 34

The prophet Amos was not a world traveler. He was not a Ph.D. He had no political influence, and was not in good standing with the powers-that-be. His appearance was probably not prepossessing, and he must have been the joke of the Bethel intelligentsia. He was utterly devoid of the qualifications for success in the courts of the capital, either civil or religious. But he had one thing going for him that all the clique of Jeroboam II were strangers to—in his humble life among his sheep and sycamores he had heard from God. He had a hot line to Headquarters and orders from the Main Office. Dr. Amaziah and all the polished gentlemen of the courts may have had the ear of the King, but they were tuned out to the Realms Above.

Maybe it is too much to expect but hope springs eternal, and we long for another Amos right out of the solitudes. Are we doomed for the rest of our days to listen to smooth experts, both in state and church, who have not had an original thought since they took office? We have had everything else, but this we have not had: a prophet like Amos from Tekoah, like John the Baptist from the wilderness, like Paul from Arabia. We have seen no candidates for their mantles, but we like to dream that one may yet break out of the woods to the consternation of all Bethelites. God speed the day!

In these days of social emphasis, we do well to remember that before God ordered His people to ". . . seek judgment, relieve the oppressed, judge the fatherless, plead for the widow" (Isaiah 1:17), He bade them, "Wash you, make you clean; put away the evil of your doings from before mine eyes; cease to do evil; Learn to do well!" (16,17). Social reform by an uncleansed and unconverted people is not the program of God.

"If ye were of the world, the world would love his own: but because ye are not of the world, but I have chosen you out of the world, therefore the world hateth you" (John 15:19). It seems to be forgotten that the church has inherited a legacy of hate from this world. By what strange twist of thinking we could ever imagine that Christians can be popular with this age is beyond me. Nothing could not be plainer than the uncompromising words of James, ". . . the friendship of the world is enmity with God . . ." (4:4).

The older generation with its premissiveness, its tolerance, its lack of discipline, has made a failure with the new theories of homelife and child training. The parents have adjusted to the children, and changed their own convictions to suit the new generation, and both old and young are going down together. Instead of molding the lives of children, the adults are now molded by the children, and the authority in the home has changed hands—however loudly it may be denied.

I was walking along, pondering the fearful events of these days, when beside my path a little white-throated sparrow began to sing. I have always loved the sweet high-pitched notes of the white-throat—so like the opening bars of the Wedding March. It made me wish I could escape these times for some serene spot—to rest in that other world all around me, of which this plaintive melody seemed to speak. But we cannot dodge these days to enjoy listening to bird songs, save for intervals when we would renew our strength. We must be in the thick of these last hours of the world's distress where the sin and sorrow are. Our Saviour moved through storm and shadow until it reached its sky-blackening, earth-shaking crescendo at Calvary. There will be plenty of time to hear white-throated sparrows when we reign with Him on a redeemed earth.

# 35

It is easy to get under the juniper like Elijah, and imagine oneself to be the Surviving Saint. God still has His seven thousand who have not bowed to Baal. And yet it is better to be jealous for the Lord of Hosts, than to be blithefully indifferent to the evils of the day. Elijah has been unduly censured. Savonarola saw "the whole world overset, all virtue and goodness disappeared, nowhere a shining light, no man taking shame for his sins." But we still remember Savonarola, and have forgotten the Happiness Boys of his time. It takes his kind to rally the Unbowed Seven Thousand in a day of apostasy, anarchy and apathy.

In Mark's account of the stilling of the tempest we read, ". . . there arose a great storm of wind" (Mark 4: 37). The disciples aroused the Lord from His sleep and we read, "And he arose . . ." (v. 39). We are in the greatest storm of history, but He is master of the storm. When the storm arises, let us arise in His strength and bid the tempest subside. Like the disciples we panic, forgetting Who is in the boat with us! We are hearing aplenty about the storm these days, but little about the Saviour. "There arose a storm. . . . and he arose."

Saul did not destroy all the Amalekites as he was told to do, but he kept King Agag and much spoil in the train of his triumph. We tend to give up ugly sins, and keep choice accursed things for ourselves. Saul tried to excuse himself by saying he had kept the best to sacrifice unto God. But God is not pleased by the sacrifices of disobedience. ". . . to obey is better than sacrifice, and to hearken than the fat of rams" (I Samuel 15:22). God cannot be bribed with a donation from the proceeds of iniquity.

"In the beginning God. . . . Where art thou . . . ? Where is . . . thy brother?" (Genesis 1:1; 3:9; 4:9). Everything begins with God. What follows is our relationship to Him and to our brother. Let a man get fixed properly in this order, and he is right both vertically and horizontally.

We organize evangelistic campaigns, and try to rally indifferent churches to cooperate in united endeavors. There are always a few in all the churches who love the Lord, and when they band together God blesses His Word, and much good is done. But how much more might happen if revived churches spontaneously filled with the Spirit outflowed and overflowed in mass evangelism! Ought we not major on reviving the churches, and then evangelism of all kinds would be a natural consequence. We are trying to have the results of revival without the revival—the effects without the cause.

Paul asked the Galatians, ". . . who hath bewitched you . . . ?" (Galatians 3:1). This is a day of sorcery, demonic deception in the end of time. The world is tricked, fascinated, under the spell of a thousand evil eyes. The weird, the uncanny, the occult, psychedelic drugs, hallucinations,—with these humanity is being swept into an orgy of induced insanity. The church is attacked, and Satan would deceive the very elect. Good men are led astray by the liberal gospel, the secular gospel, the social gospel. Jannes and Jambres imitate Moses. The Great Deceiver as an angel of light imitates every work of God, and thousands of poor souls cannot distinguish wheat from tares. Fortune-tellers, necromancers, magicians, are small fry compared to the new witchery let loose upon the world. Men we never dreamed would weaken are giving way, and Satan has so cleverly maneuvered his strategy that it appears unchristian to lift a voice against his wiles and devices. This procedure is so skillfully executed, that many are afraid to express even doubt of it,—much less opposition. We had better take some special courses in Ephesians Six, and learn the true nature of spiritual conflict. We have been provided full equipment for this warfare, and we had better learn how to evaluate both our adversaries and our allies.

# 36

I would say to today's young minister, "Be not afraid to give much time to solitary walks and meditation. You can well afford to dispense with many other activities some may think indispensable. You will be returning to a way of life almost forgotten now, and you may be eyed askance by all runners in the Great Rat Race. But your chance may come one day to speak your piece on some strategic occasion, when weary humanity has reached saturation and boredom listening to everything else. On that day, your quiet walks and lonely vigils will pay off. If that chance never comes, they have paid off anyway.

Our Lord said to the church at Smyrna: "I know thy . . . tribulation" (Revelation 2:9). The word means "pressure." He also said, ". . . In the world ye shall have tribulation [pressure]" (John 16:33). "Pressure" is a much-used word nowadays. We are all under pressure. Some explode under it, and end up in mental hospitals. We have pressurized cookers and pressurized cabins. The Communists brainwash their victims under the torture of demonic pressure. Even preachers are pressurized by ecclesiastical authorities, the system, the demands of their churches. Some give way; the prophet becomes a priest— a prisoner of conformity, a parrot, a rubber stamp, a yes-man—pressurized into a pitiful puppet.

"Be not squeezed into the mold of this age" is my interpretation of Romans 12:2. And that is another way of saying, "Don't be pressurized into the pattern of this world!"

It is never wise to use as a sermon text a verse that begins with *And*. If we confine ourselves to that text, we have not said all that God meant to say in that connection. For instance, we often hear sermons from the verse, ". . . Ye shall know the truth and the truth shall make you free" (John 9:32). But the first word in the verse is "And" which indicates that something has gone before. The preceding verse says, ". . . If ye continue in my word, then are ye my disciples indeed." Then follows, "And ye shall know the truth and the truth shall make you free." Likewise, we hear sermons from Romans 12:2 about being not conformed to the word, but the preceding verse bids us present our bodies as living sacrifices. First, the positive, then the negative nonconformity to the world, and finally the positive again, "Be ye transformed." We must have the whole passage to give a complete message. Torn out of context, one verse does not say all that God has said on that matter. We must preach not only the truth and nothing but the truth, but *the whole truth* in a given passage.

It would seem by now that common sense and ordinary intelligence would convince us that trying to negotiate with Communism is a waste of time. For years we have sat at tables trying to play with a team of demonized men who play by no rules but their own. Months of haggling in Paris settled nothing but the shape of the conference table. England's Chamberlain found that he couldn't do business with a demoniac by the name of Hitler. The times called for a Churchill. Peaceful coexistence is no more possible with the devil than with cancer. Satan goes about as a roaring lion, and you can't talk thngs over with a lion. The only match for the *demon*-stration is found in a *demonstration* of the Holy Spirit. Only He is a match for the devil, and it is to be feared that our diplomats are not sufficiently endowed with Pentecostal power to cope with demonism. Ordinary human wit is totally inadequate to wrestle with the powers of darkness, whether in our individual lives or in the State Department.

## 37

*The Church Bought, ". . . purchased with his own blood"* (Acts 20:28).
*The Church Beset without and within* (v.29).
*The Church Blessed, commended to God and the word of His grace* (v.32).

The decisive battle of a war usually comes near the end, but the Christian's victory was won long ago at the death and resurrection of our Lord. Our Waterloo is behind us, and we are engaged in mopping-up operations. Of course the ultimate consummation comes at His return and our resurrection, and meanwhile, we live in His victory day by day. But the historians do not recognize that the really decisive moment of history is behind us nearly twenty centuries.

God saved us to make us holy, not happy. Some experiences may not contribute to our happiness, but all can be made to contribute to our holiness.

It is not enough to wake up—we must get up. Some

Christians are temporarily aroused, only to turn over and go back to sleep. Moreover, we must stay up, ". . . for they that sleep, sleep in the night . . . but we . . . are of the day . . ." (I Thessalonians 5:7, 8).

A pastor met one of his delinquent members on the street. "I haven't seen you at church lately," he reminded him.

"No," was the reply, "We've had sickness, and then the weather has been so bad. You know it has rained and rained and rained."

"But it's always dry at church."

"Yes," came the answer, "and that's another reason why I've not been coming!"

No church service should be dry, dull and lifeless. Worship was never meant to be entertaining, but it should be alive and vivid with the presence of God.

There is a mass stampede away from responsibility. Very few really want to work, and fewer still take pride in their work. We are buck-passers in the age of the half-done job. But our Lord rewards us for the well-done job. Church members can be counted, but how few can be counted upon! We have counted numbers, but numbers do not count. Yet the one supreme requirement of our Lord is not brilliance or success, but plain old-fashioned faithfulness. It is fast disappearing in the home, in business, in the workshop, in church. Everybody yells for his rights, but is silent about his responsibilities. There is nothing Hollywood about dependability, but it is the greatest of all abilities.

Now that we have split the atom, reached the moon, and discovered DNA, our exports are preparing to tackle our moral problems. The technologists will turn theologians, and mechanics will devise morals. It is about time, of course, to do something about the spiritual, for while man's body soars to the skies, his soul slumps in the slime. But if these gentlemen imagine that they can play God, and handle the things of the spirit like they can put parts of a machine together, they are in for a big surprise. Working with a machine is one thing, but tinkering with man himself is something else. This is another world, and the problem was met and solved long ago by Jesus Christ. When men rush in here where angels fear to tread, they prepare the way for Antichrist, who will ". . . opposeth and exalteth himself above all that is called God, or that is worshipped; so that he as God sitteth in the temple of God, shewing himself that he is God" (2 Thessalonians 2:4).

# 38

It is now becoming the fashion for government to sign confessions and make apologies in order to secure the release of prisoners. After the release, the confession is repudiated as a lie. Few eyebrows will be lifted, for lying is now accepted as a part of our way of life. The excuse is the worn old argument that the end justifies the means. We have long used that alibi to explain other practices, and since things grow worse spontaneously if they are not corrected designedly, we are not surprised at the degeneracy that believes in doing evil in order to do good.

"God is a Spirit: and they that worship him must worship Him in spirit and in truth" (John 4:24). The church member who sits grudgingly at church wishing he were somewhere else might as well be somewhere else. No wife appreciates the attentions of a husband when she knows his mind is on another woman with whom he would rather be. James calls adulterers and adulteresses those who love the world, and are therefore at enmity with God. He who sits in church from a mere sense of duty when the heart is at home watching a favorite TV show, might as well have watched it. He is not worshiping God in spirit and truth, when he would prefer worshiping at the shrine of some actress with the face of an angel and the morals of an alley cat.

Some confess Christ as Saviour who have never submitted to Him as Lord. Some acknowledge Him as Saviour and Lord who do not know Him as their Life. He is our life, and the only true life a Christian has is the indwelling Christ within Him. I do not mean we must move through three successive stages knowing Christ as Saviour, Lord and Life. He is Everything—Alpha and Omega and all the alphabet between. Few Christians, however, seem to know anything about the constant and conscious experience of the Living Christ by faith for every need of body, mind and spirit. This is the vine branch relationship, and all we are and do is simply the outliving of the inliving Christ. The Christian life is not merely a matter of living like or for Christ. Paul said, "To me to live is Christ . . ." (Philippians 1:21). The Christian life *is* Christ living in and through us by our consent and with our cooperation.

There is no greater hindrance to revival than a comfortable pastor settled and satisfied, coasting along until he reaches retirement, who does not want his flock disturbed or the status quo upset. He has long since lost his burden and concern for a mighty upheaval of

God among the resters at ease in Zion. He resents any intrusion into the complacency of a sleeping church, and interprets the prophet's call to repentance as an indictment of his own preaching. He is determined not to get excited, assumes a philosophical tolerance of things as they are, and he may speak facetiously of the prophet's seriousness. Sometimes his own people may get under conviction, and put him to shame by a concern he does not seem to feel. This makes it exceedingly difficult for any revivalist calling Christians to repentance, but what a delight when pastor and prophet stand together! Most pastors understand that the traveling prophet can say things the pastor cannot say—that he fills a different role, and follows an utterly different pattern. They complement each other. One plants, another waters, but God gives the increase. The teacher plants the seed, the pastor cultivates the crop, the evangelist gathers it, but the prophet must first break up the fallow ground. Breaking up ground is never a pleasant comfortable business, and churches sometimes resent the plow of plain preaching. Blessed is the pastor who knows this, and stands behind the lonely prophet who calls the church to repentance.

# 39

After listening to some of our popular singers these days, we are convinced that it is not necessary to know how to sing in order to sell a million records. It may be that singers who can't sing are making more money that those who can. Any tomcat on a back fence in the summertime could wail at better pitch than some celebrities on TV. The average popular song nowadays is not music to begin with, and the performer couldn't sing it even if it were. Neither musical ability nor training is necessary to reach stardom. Other qualifications, like appearance and sex appeal, do figure, but the one thing not required is that one know how to sing.

This has gotten over into the world of religion. Worship has become a performance instead of an experience. The notion has spread, somehow, that the Gospel must be made into a form of entertainment. Some have discovered that a fortune can be made out of religious jazz. Sacred themes have been prostituted into hillbilly ragtime, and the same performers who turn out sexy ads also produce sacred albums. Athletic and theatrical prowess draw out crowds who would never go to hear a mere preacher, and evangelists may have to add sideburns, medallions and a *git-tar* to guarantee a congregation. The churches, even in dignified circles, are working out a coalition with the world to popularize the Gospel.

The New Testament is loaded with *Therefores*. Check your concordance and you will be amazed. Hebrews, for instance, is constantly saying, "*Let us, therefore...*" Because of all that Christ has done for us, and is to us, *Therefore* we ought to give the more earnest heed; we ought to fear lest we come short of His rest; let us go on unto perfection; let us come boldly to the throne of grace; let us draw near; let us go unto Him without the camp. Paul writes, "Having therefore these promises, ... let us cleanse ourselves..." (2 Corintheans 7:1), and "I beseech you therefore, ... present your bodies..." (Romans 12:1). These are only samples of a constantly recurring summons. The mercies of God, the promises of God, are not sweet morsels to roll under our tongues; they are meant to be heavenly stimulants to stir us to action. They are not lullabies, but reveilles. Too many sleeping disciples need to hear our Lord's word in the Garden, "Rise, let us be going..." (Matthew 26:46).

This morning the mother of a fourteen-year-old-son said to me," This is the first time he has ever wanted to come hear a preacher, but this week during these meetings he has asked to come to church." Last night a youngster, probably about eight, said to me, "I got a lot out of your sermon." I have better attention and response today than in all my fifty-five years of preaching. The idea that we must cheapen the Gospel, and put on a show to interest youth is nonsense. They are fed up with sham and the distracted efforts of older folks to interest them. Straight talk that hits hard will attract more than all the silly and pitiful stunts of churches in the show business.

In Luke (14:26, 27) our Lord says in effect, that if any man comes to Him and comes not after Him, he cannot be His disciple. It is true that He said, . . . "him that cometh to me, I will in no wise cast out" (John 6:37), but we must mean business. We must come to Him with the intention and purpose to follow Him. The step must become a walk. Crisis must be followed by continuance. Matriculation must be followed by taking His yoke, and becoming His disciple. We must love Him so that all other loves are as hatred in comparison; we must bear our cross, and forsake all we have, as He declared in the three "cannots" in Luke (14:25-33). We have invited people to come to Jesus, but we have touched lightly on coming after Him. Therefore in our churches we have many members, but few disciples.

# 40

The Scriptures speak of the water of life, the bread of life, spiritual meat, and the milk of the Word. Water and bread and meat and milk are basic; they are staples. They are not hors d'ouvres or appetizers or desserts. Too many pulpits have gone into the knickknack business, dispensing finger sandwiches and cream puffs. We are told that in the last days men will not endure sound doctrine, so now we have finicky congregations who cannot take solid substantial fare. Their jaded appetites must be tickled with tidbits. The big question is, Shall we give them what they want or what they need? Pitiful sermonettes, Gospel jazz and all the cute little tricks the church has resorted to in order that this TV generation may be pleased and entertained—all this is a surrender to a generation fed at the delicatessen instead of in the dining room. It is no wonder that we have a sick church, considering its diet. Back to bread and meat and milk!

The men God has used to revive His work have been concerned and burdened about their times. Amos spoke of those who were not grieved for the affliction of Joseph.

Jeremiah, in tears for the state of his people, asked, "Is it nothing to you, all ye that pass by?" (Lamentations, 1:12). Paul could wish himself accursed for his Jewish brethren. John Knox prayed, "Give me Scotland or I die!" Evan Roberts lived in prayer for revival. Blithe clergymen, cracking jokes and whistling their way past the graveyard, will see no visitation of God. The situation is desperate, but the saints are not. America is in her gravest danger, but Americans are laughing themselves to death watching TV clowns. Any minister with a heavy heart for the sins of the church is actually dubbed a Jeremiah. No revival ever started in fun and frivolity. God is on the lookout for someone who really cares.

Nothing has been overworked more in defense of questionable practices today than the Scripture about Jesus eating with publicans and sinners. All sorts of hobnobbing with Sodom and getting chummy with Gomorrah have been justified by our Saviour's presence at wedding feasts with some of the socially untouchables of His time. The facts are that He came first to the lost sheep of the house of Israel. He came unto His own, and His own received Him not. He presented the Kingdom to Israel, and in the first part of His ministry shared their simple social life. But as He drew nearer to the cross, and His own refused Him, there was less socializing until He ate the last supper only with His disciples, and after His Resurrection he fellowshipped only with His own. The Acts presents no such practice, and it shows up nowhere through the rest of the New Testament. It served a particular need at a particular time, and was never meant to be stretched to cover cocktail parties at country clubs today.

We are accustomed to think of church revival in emotional terms—loud preaching, enthusiastic singing, excitement. Finney's classic definition still stands, "Whereas mind and conscience may assent to truth, when revival comes, obedience to the truth is the one thing that matters. Revival is nothing less than a new beginning of obedience to God." This is why many so-called revivals fail. When the excitement subsides, nothing remains. When Christians are truly revived, they begin a new life of submission to Christ and obedience to God's Word and will. Excitement, ecstasy, rejoicing, may accompany this decision but, feeling or no feeling, it issues in ". . . patient continuance in well-doing" (Romans 2:7).

We remember the Cheshire cat in Alice's adventures. The cat had a grin that remained in the air after the cat had disappeared. Some think we conservatives are dour and stern, but there is at least more substance to the cat without the grin than to the grin without the cat. The new school of churchless Christianity, that decries dogma in favor of dialogue, fits neatly into the Cheshire category.